STILL DOING

T0363736

Professor Tina Koch (RN, PhD) holds a joint appointment between Flinders University and the Royal District Nursing Service.

Dr Merilyn Annells (RN, PhD) is a research consultant who was contracted for this 'positive ageing' project.

Marina Brown (RN, BN) is a research assistant at the Royal District Nursing Service, South Australia.

STILL DOING

Twelve men talk about ageing

edited by
Tina Koch, Merilyn Annells
and Marina Brown

Wakefield
Press

Wakefield Press
17 Rundle Street
Kent Town
South Australia 5067

First published 1999
Reprinted 2000

Cover photograph of Kym Bonython by Mick Bradley
Cover design by Liz Nicholson, design BITE
Designed and typeset by Clinton Ellicott, Wakefield Press
Printed and bound by Hyde Park Press, Adelaide

National Library of Australia
Cataloguing-in-publication entry

Koch, Tina.
Still doing, twelve Australian men talk about ageing.

ISBN 1 86254 497 2.
1. Aged men – Australia – Interviews. 2. Aged men –
Australia – Attitudes. 3. Aging – Australia. I. Annells, Merilyn.
II. Brown, Marina. III. Title.

305.260994

'And still be doing, never done ...'

Hudibras, Samuel Butler

CONTENTS

EDITORS' NOTE

We gratefully acknowledge the Royal District Nursing Service Foundation of South Australia for their generosity toward the production of this book.

Thank you to Shannon Kantji and Piero Merindi for their services as interpreters for the interviews of *tjilpi* Kantji and Vincenzo Perrini respectively. We appreciate the advice and assistance of Eve Lynch, Sandra Ken, Eileen Willis, Connie Perrini, and Franca Antonello.

Our gratitude is extended to all those people who suggested men who were ageing positively in South Australia. Most of all, we appreciate the invaluable contribution of the twelve men who agreed to participate in the positive ageing project, and who also agreed to their stories being published in this book. It was a privilege to meet and talk with you.

FOREWORD

Colin Thiele

Some of the boys of my childhood tended to regard old people as desiccated relics of a bygone age – grandma in her rocking chair with gently clicking knitting needles, grandpa peering myopically at the newspaper through thick lensed glasses.

Even in those distant days such stereotypes were inaccurate. Most of the men I knew still worked out in the paddocks in their seventies and eighties, and women of even greater age performed prodigies in the farmyard and kitchen. While there was work to be done they did it. True to the title of this book they were 'still doing'.

Unhappily the perception of age as a period of uselessness peopled by old drones having nothing to contribute and nothing to say has persisted down the years and still exists in some places. (Shakespeare's seven ages of man in *As You Like It* didn't help with its dismal picture of the 'lean and slippered pantaloon' finally fading into second childishness 'sans teeth, sans eyes, sans taste, sans everything'.)

Luckily that view is countered by countless examples in history of the great achievements of older men and women: Wordsworth still writing actively in his late seventies, Verdi composing grandly in his eighties ... The stories of the twelve in this book encourage us all to follow that tradition as we ourselves grow older. Despite the diversity of their careers and interests common threads bind them – strength of spirit, mental vigour, ongoing involvement with life. Their message is clear. 'Don't vegetate. Keep doing.'

The Royal District Nursing Service of South Australia, and the compilers and publishers of this collection, are to be congratulated on making such a worthwhile contribution to the International Year of the Older Person.

PREFACE

Chances are that when an ordinary Aussie (assuming that there is such a person) hears the words 'older man', an image will flash to mind of a relatively inactive and not necessarily happy individual. Think for a moment about the numerous adjectives that are commonly used to describe older men, like 'slow', or 'grumpy', as in the film title. Generally the adjectives are not very complimentary, unless Father Christmas is the image, and even his existence is disputed!

We, the three members of the project team (Tina Koch, Merilyn Annells and Marina Brown), understand that altering community attitudes is not easy, but we do believe that stories of positive ageing assist in the recognition, respect, and realistic portrayal of older men.

The idea for this project arose from Tina Koch's earlier PhD work which involved discussions with older people in a hospital ward. The patients explained how the ageism of their caregivers was profoundly and negatively influencing the way they were considered and treated. They felt depersonalised.

So, the actual aim of the book is to challenge the various negative stereotypes that exist about older men. In another book, *Still Me*, we have aimed to do likewise for negative stereotypes of older women.

In this, the International Year of Older Persons, twelve South Australian men were selected to be interviewed for this book about their experiences of ageing. It will become obvious how diverse a group of men they are. Their interests, priorities, experiences, activities, circumstances, and attitudes vary, but it is apparent that the men are all 'doers'. They explain that they are still doing things that they want to do, that they enjoy doing. Purposely remaining active, they are a fairly happy and content mob, as you will read. All are examples of positive ageing – they are an inspiration.

It was no easy matter to limit this book to the stories of just twelve Australian men who are ageing 'well'. From our own brainstorming, the initial list that we compiled was very long, and when we started to ask around for other suggestions, a huge list resulted. It took considerable effort to limit the list to twelve men. Many others could have been included.

Some of the men are well-known personalities and privileged public figures, but there are also those who are not prominent Australians. The age range is from sixty-five to eighty-eight. It is difficult to satisfactorily define 'aged' or 'older', as the terms are rather relative – we are all ageing and older in comparison with others. However, as Australian men can apply for an aged pension following their sixty-fifth birthday, we chose that as the minimum age for prospective interviewees. One of the men, *tjilpi* Kanytji, is of unknown age, but reasonable estimates place him well into his seventies, or even his eighties.

The interviews tended to follow issues raised by the men, but no doubt the questions and body language of the inter-viewer influenced the foci and content of the interview. By analysing transcripts of the tape-recorded interviews, we members of the project team came to agree on the significant points and themes of each interview. These points and themes directed which parts of the interview were to be included in that man's chapter, which in most cases, because of space constraints, is a condensed version of the interview. Finally, each of the men perused a draft of his chapter, and additions, deletions, or alterations were negotiated until he gave permission for the publication of the chapter.

We recognise that when reading an interview, it is often helpful to be aware of the interview milieu. Therefore we include a summary description of each interview's place and surroundings.

We have deliberately compiled the following twelve interviews in a style that will result in you feeling that you are listening to each man tell his story. Many of the idiosyncrasies of spoken English, as recorded in the interviews, have been preserved. The style and formality of the writing would be vastly different if the men had been asked to write their stories, rather than tell their story in a conversational interview.

We hope this will be an interesting read. At the end of the stories, in a concluding chapter, we discuss our interpretations of the diversity and intriguing similarities between the interviews.

Tina Koch, Merilyn Annells and Marina Brown

HORSE HOBBY

Colin Hayes

Colin Hayes died on Friday 21 May 1999, several months after this interview took place. He was praised by former Prime Minister Bob Hawke as one of the greatest figures in the Australian racing industry, and a marvellous human being and friend. Colin received the Order of Australia Medal, and also the Order of the British Empire for outstanding service to the racing industry. With no tradition of racing in his family, Colin rose from the status of amateur jockey to an amazing forty-year 'track record'. This record includes training 5333 winners, achieving 41 premierships, the most winners in a season from 1989–90, with also the most stake money, plus the most group and listed winners, in that same season. World records include ten winners in a day (23/1/82), five group winners in a day (7/2/87), and six black-type winners in a day (12/9/87).

Retired from a very successful career as a horse trainer, Colin lived with his wife at the white-fenced family property and horse stud, Lindsay Park, situated on rolling hills outside Angaston, in the Barossa Valley. He spoke to us from his armchair surrounded by photographs of horses, paintings of racing scenes and trophies.

Well, if your hobby is your work, your life goes very quickly. Horses have always been my hobby, so I find it hard to believe that I'm seventy-five. I still run the companies and the stud. The horses are my love and passion.

Breeding horses is very exciting when it's spring and the new foals are dropping. I still get a big buzz seeing how they look and which way they're thrown, and then planning their development. I suppose, to me, that side of things gives fulfilment, particularly if you think that you have bred a good one. It keeps me very interested – the planning of the matings, the bloodlines, the breeding and nutrition programs, and developing the foals. I suppose I've been lucky because it's been my hobby and it is also my work.

Lindsay Park, which I own, has developed a reputation for producing 'winners', both at training and at breeding. I get a lot of satisfaction from that, of course. With the breeding record we are getting up toward 13,000 races.

I retired from actual training when I was sixty-six. My sons do the training now. As a trainer, I led in two states, South Australia and Victoria. As a breeder, we have done very well. To me it was because I built connections and contacts. People were starting to rely on my judgement and business. I found that was so from about when I was fifty to when I retired. Since then we have held it, with the help of the boys and the family.

A lot of people like to retire, but if you don't have to retire, I don't think you should. I've kept myself vitally interested in my profession. When I retired from training, I was the Vice-Chairman of the TAB. When I retired from that after three years, I was an initial member of the Australian Sports Commission, representing the sport of racing. That was all after retirement. I think it is very important that you keep your mind working.

I try to do everything that I used to, except when my body lets me know that I can't. I can't because I have had a couple of open-heart operations and I have a few other problems. I had my first cardiac operation at fifty-one, and the next one when I was fifty-six. But those years, between fifty and sixty, were my most productive years. I achieved more then than any time before.

I find that with getting older, as long as you stay within the limits that nature allows you, you can handle it. It all revolves around your health, really. If I stress myself too much, I get angina. I fractured my back when I was about eighteen, on a buck-jumper, and that has given me osteoarthritis in the back, which affects the sciatic nerve and all those things, and if I have to stand up for too long, I'm in trouble. So, I have to recognise that and live with it. It keeps my physical activities down to a minimum.

If I find that I'm getting very tired, or that I'm getting too many little problems, I stop and rest a bit, where before I didn't. Before, I only ever slept six hours and worked the rest. I've always had a big capacity for work, but now I have a rest every day after lunch, and then I sleep about seven hours at night. I'm always awake and ready to go out by about six o'clock in the morning, because nature tunes your body that way I think.

I see all the fast gallops at the tracks in the morning with my sons, Peter and David, if they are here. I watch the fast work-up and I try not to look over their shoulder too hard, but if they need any help, then I'm there. It works very well. Peter is a leading trainer here and David is a leading trainer in Hong Kong. My sons are different, but they do ask me about things when they are in doubt. Mostly though, I encourage them to make their own decisions. Anybody who is older and who thinks he has got all the answers is crazy. It's a changing world and you have to adapt.

It wasn't hard to hand over the training to the boys. It was the right time and I had planned it carefully. I thought about it quite a bit because I didn't want anything disrupting the clients' confidence. Peter, at the time, didn't want the stress of it all and he went away on his own for a while, so I bought him a property and helped him. Peter is a private person but is proving an excellent trainer and I'm very proud of him.

When I did hand over, I knew that David would handle it very well, and he has. He has an amazing record as a trainer. I said at the time that I would get more enjoyment out of watching my sons break my records than I did when I made them. And they have done just that, you know, so it has been very good really.

David will have to buy Peter out when I go. So, David said to me, 'Dad, with the low taxation and the great rewards in Hong Kong, I would like to go to Hong Kong.' This was when he was top of the tree here. He had won every decent race from the Melbourne Cup, the Caulfield Cup, to the Sydney and the Tokyo Cup (which an Australian had never won before). He broke the Commonwealth record for winners.

So he was right at the top of the tree and he said, 'I am sure I could make more progress and have the money to pay Peter out.' Peter agreed to come back then. It was quite an amiable discussion and we thrashed it all out, you know. We had a family meeting and I could see what David was trying to do. He will eventually come home, as he wants his children to go to school in Australia. His wife is a lovely girl. They had a boy and a girl, and then they had twin boys who are now three years old.

I've been so busy with the property, keeping it all going.

Lindsay Park was part of the original land grant of South Australia in 1838. George Fife Angas was really the founding father of South Australia, and this was his property and house. It had not changed hands from the Angas family until I bought it in 1965. It took me five years to get it set up – tracks and all that sort of thing. I used to train at Semaphore and the beach was very nice, but I put a swimming pool in here and our records improved quickly, with the rural setting.

We came here to live in 1970. The house has three elevations and we now live upstairs where there is a back entrance. When I had my first heart operation Betty had that done. We use the hill so we don't have three flights of stairs to walk up. We can park the car at the back usually, and just walk in.

The foundations of the house were put down in 1840. For this part of the world, it is an historical site. The stone was all quarried on the property – marble and sandstone. The English Oak panelling inside came as ballast in the ships. Lady Angas had the panels painted pastel green, as just after the war pastel shades came in. It looked quite attractive but Betty brought the panelling back to the wood. It is a lovely old house.

Moving to Lindsay Park created and built a new way of life for our family, which has been very rewarding and very happy. Our family all live around us, apart from David. They are all involved in the business with us.

Betty has said to one of our daughters, 'What do you think is the thing that keeps your father going?' This may sound a bit egotistical, but I don't mean it that way. She said: 'His wisdom. He has got such common sense.' If any of the children have problems they come to me, and I talk to them, but they have been lucky with their children.

We have four children and fifteen grandchildren. I just had two of the grandchildren here to stay. They had been in

America for some time over Christmas with their American family, then came home full of enthusiasm for life. They give you another aspect, you know! Their father is an American and he runs Angas Park, the dried fruit company, of which I'm the major shareholder. I'm on the board there with him. It's a family company, and he has developed it into the biggest dried fruit company in Australia, with three hundred employees. So that is a big interest and has opened up a new world for me.

I remember when the grandchildren's mother, one of my daughters, was about ten. I took her to the pet shop and gave her the pick of all the dogs. She chose a crossbred terrier that was an awful looking dog. I asked, 'Why that one, Kerrie?' and she said, 'I think it needs me.' So, I bought it for her and it became an unbelievable pet, as those crossbreeds can be – intensely loyal and intelligent.

Kerrie trained as a nurse at the Royal Adelaide Hospital. When she graduated, she came home and took the dog with her when she went down the street. It was a hot day, so she wound the car window down a bit for the dog to get plenty of air while she ran across the street. But the dog squeezed through to follow her, and a car hit him. The dog was then about eleven years old because Kerrie was twenty-one.

Along came this American man and helped her with the injured dog and they brought him back here to our vet, but they had to put him down. Well, the American took her out to dinner that night, and twelve months later they were married. Now they have four beautiful children. I said at the wedding that she should treat him like her dog: feed him well, plenty of affection, a little leash, and he will always come home. It's worked. They get on beautifully and they are very happy. I think that you are lucky if you have a close family.

My other daughter, Jan, the eldest, her husband runs a

farm for me. He is a lovely bloke. He was born in Austria, but he came out here when he was about five or six. They have two lovely children. The eldest is a girl about twenty-five who is married to a farmer. She lives down at Bordertown, but that's not that far away, you know.

Our children have all grown very close. The bonding happened very early, and that's mainly due to their mother, of course. Betty has been fantastic with them all. She has been very unselfish in everything that she has done. Because I was so busy, the way our children were reared, and the way they grew, did depend mostly upon their mother's influence. I find that I'm a better grandparent than I was a parent. I have always been close to the children, but I think that as a grandparent you have more time to give, and it's very rewarding.

I think that, as you get older, you get more, I don't mean 'soft', but more able to understand their problems. You become much more tolerant and understanding of somebody else's problems.

I'm still on one committee, the Onkaparinga Racing Club Committee. I tried to retire but they wouldn't let me. They are lovely people and friends. I actually enjoy it. Also, I enjoy keeping an interest in the track. You can't go cold on it. Now I enjoy the boys' success most, though.

The training business was started from scratch. It was good to build it. As I've said, it was my hobby. I didn't have time to play golf, although I used to play sport a bit once (tennis, football, and cricket), but I had to give it away; horses became totally dominating. I had to give them my full concentration.

I enjoy watching the cricket and I watch the tennis. During the football season I follow South Australian teams, but I don't particularly go, as television makes life much easier these days. As far as sport goes, physically I can't do it much now. I can't play bowls, or do the things that a lot of other people do.

I'm an avid reader of anything to do with horses, a bit singular that way, but I do enjoy a good read now and then of sporting books. I enjoyed Richie Benaud's book recently. I've trained horses for a lot of those people who are written about. I love the things that he wrote and to which I can relate, because I've had insight through having been trainer for the horses of some of the best sportsmen. Golfers, tennis players, cricketers, footballers – over the years, all of them, at some stage of my life.

You reminisce a bit, I suppose. You remember the funny things that happened. Jack Kramer, a famous American tennis player who started professional tennis, had a manager in Australia called Bob Barnes, who was a friend of mine. Bob was 'one off' being a Davis Cup player himself. He used to run any business interests that Jack had in Australia.

Well, they decided that they wanted to gamble. So we had a plan where they took a horse to Brisbane and ran him up there. Then they took the horse to Sydney, where they were all based. They had this gamble. We ran it first up at Canterbury and the favourite was an English horse trained by Tommy Smith. Our horse was called Trackmaster, and we took Bill Pyers, our champion jockey at the time, up to Sydney to ride it. Ted Harris, who is still a prominent businessman today, had the job of getting Bill to the race fit, which was no mean feat in those days. Bill was probably the best jockey who ever rode for me.

The race was run and we burst to front and opened up a gap of four or five lengths at Canterbury, which is a very short run. Bob Barnes couldn't contain himself, he was shaking hands with strangers saying, 'We've won. We've won it.' Next thing he came to his father-in-law, and his father-in-law said, 'You fool, it has run out of the gate!' As our horse got to the winning post, it veered out. So it was a photo finish, but we did win.

They had worked it very carefully. The late Lew Hoad, the famous tennis player, had to put the money on ten minutes before the race with this special bookmaker. So, they all rushed back to Bob Barnes' house at Randwick, where Hoady was. They found him asleep by the phone, with a can of beer beside him. They shook him awake and he asked, 'What time is it?' He had slept right through the race, despite all the planning that we did for six months, and he hadn't put the money on! He slept right through. Lew was a lovely bloke, and we soon forgave him.

When I was young, we had horses in the family, but no racing people. I knew what I wanted and I loved horses. I had an instant rapport with them, an instant memory for them. If I saw a horse running in a crowd, then I'd know it was one with which I had been acquainted. I could catch horses that nobody else could catch. Little things like that. I concentrated on their eyes. You don't know that you are doing it, as you do it automatically. You out-psyche them, more or less. Some people have it, others never get it.

I think it is important to have the ability to notice changes in a horse's behaviour. A horse can have certain characteristics and you notice that he is not acting right. You can look and tell if he needs a gallop or doesn't need a gallop. There is no rule to it. It is something that is more an art than a science, put it that way. You do the bonding when they are very young and you sort of become close to them.

Also, animals are more trusting of some people than other people. Anybody with too short a fuse is very hard on the animals. We don't employ them or we soon get rid of them. You learn who to employ to work with the horses. We have staff who have been here since I bought the place, and we have other staff who have been with me longer. Some of their sons and grandchildren are working for me now. Harrie Ling, my secretary, started school with me. He is about ten months younger than I am, and we are still friends.

Dulcify was the best racehorse I have ever had. He was a cheap horse I bought for $3250 in New Zealand, and he proved to be Australia's champion. He was killed in the Melbourne Cup when he was a short-price favourite. Dulcify was a superlative horse and provided my happiest moments with these absolutely brilliant finishes. My saddest moment was when he was killed.

I have had so many good horses. The very first racehorse I ever had was Surefoot who was bought for nine pounds from a chap selling rodeo horses near the saleyards at Gepps Cross. The horses had come down from the station country. This chap wanted ten pounds, but I only had nine, so we tossed for it, and I won. I took Surefoot home by leading him off my bicycle.

In those days I used to ride as an amateur, and at one event at Cheltenham I put all my honeymoon money on Surefoot, each-way at 66/1. During the race, it didn't look hopeful. As the barrier went up, we stumbled when another horse went under Surefoot's neck, then we had to catch up with the rest of the field, which was almost out of sight. I just kept using hands and heels, as he was a thin-skinned horse who would not respond to the whip. He still had five horses in front when we reached the straight. We kept at it though, and he got up to run third at the post. Our honeymoon was saved! Surefoot was like a pal to me and we really came along together. I learnt the business with him.

My first client was a man called Otto Heysen, the brother of Hans Heysen, the famous artist. He was a tiny fellow, as quick as a flash, who lived until he was in his nineties. I met him when he was seventy-two. We used to race in partnership and I trained all sorts of horses for him. We became very good friends. I remember him coming down to the stable one day, when he was eighty-odd, and saying, 'I reckon I can still get on that horse.' He couldn't, but he tried. Once, when he was pushing ninety, he came to New Zealand with us. He said: 'I'll never give up. You have to just stay and mix with everybody just the same. Keep your mind active.' I thought he had a great attitude to old age.

Probably the best moment in my career was winning the first Melbourne Cup. It had been such an unlucky race for me. The year before I had Dulcify, the short-price favourite, killed in it. I had a horse called Clear Prince run third in it, severing a tendon in the process. I had several placings that should have won, and didn't. I thought, 'Gee, am I ever going to win this race?'

Then, in 1980, we ran a horse in the race that Robert Sangster sent out, Beldale Ball, that was a stone below the others, and I 'cranked it up' as far as ability went. He had forty-nine kilos, was a five-year-old, but could stay. I had him fit on the day and he got all the breaks in the race. He won. That was my first Melbourne Cup. The second one was At Talaq (1986). I did expect that horse to win, as he was a very good horse. So I've won two Melbourne Cups and David's won one. We've had three trained off these gallops that I designed. Better Loosen Up was a very good horse too that I trained and handed over to David. He won the Japan Cup with it.

I don't think it matters allowing overseas horses to enter the Melbourne Cup. We don't limit the tennis players! If you want the best horse, and if it's a handicapped race, it would be good to get a lightweight. I think it has made it a very universal race.

Unfortunately though, I have seen the racing industry here, in South Australia, withering on the vine. The government has bled it and bled it and bled it, because various factions have never been able to widen their vision. Right now we are trying to come up with ideas to revitalise the industry in South Australia. It is booming in other states, but not here. We used to be the second leading breeding state and now we are right down the bottom, because nobody has bought any new mares and the incentives are missing. The last sports minister, Graham Ingerson, did try. For an industry that is such a huge employer, and with so much money in it, it is a shame. It needs someone with a lot more vision and a lot more strength to pull it into place because it not only touches on horses and gambling, but on the transport industry, the fodder industry, the textile industry, et cetera.

Also there is the proposed GST. While it may be good for the economy, it's not good for our industry. For instance, they can say taking the duty off this, or removing the various indirect taxes that we have got to pay for different things, offsets it, but fodder isn't taxed for horse expenses anyway. So you would have to pay ten per cent more for fodder. Everything is ten per cent more. If you sell a horse, you have got to get the person to pay ten per cent more all the time, as there is no way you can discount it or work it back. It is going to be very difficult. Thinking people in the industry are very concerned. It's made life very difficult for New Zealanders, and it will have the same effect here, if the government gets it through.

I've travelled overseas every year for years – for thirty years, I suppose. Mostly it was to make overseas contacts. We introduced the Arabs to Australia, you know – the sheiks. We were also able to bring Robert Sangster and some of the biggest names in the industry here.

Soon we are going on a tour on the *QE2* for the best part of three weeks. It goes first to Fremantle, then to Bali, Brunei, Manila, and then across to Hong Kong. So David, Pru and their children will meet us there. We will have a few days with them, and then we fly home. We don't travel much these days, as I prefer to stay home as much as I can, but it will be good to see the family. Also, a trip on the *Queen Elizabeth* is, from what I hear, something exceptional.

I keep my mind working. You don't do well if you let yourself vegetate. There are lots of ways that people can keep themselves active with all sorts of things. I have friends in my age group who still work for charities and still do things, and they are the ones who are doing well. Some people age so much better than others; those who are doing better are motivated. They want to do something, and they find things to do. Motivation is a very important thing.

There are not many good things about being older, I can tell you. You are kidding yourself if you say otherwise. If you are honest with yourself, you recognise that you are a bit limited, physically particularly. If you don't recognise it, you are stupid. If that is why people retire, I don't have any problem with that.

Coping with being older comes back to keeping your mind active and not losing interest in what is happening around you. It doesn't matter what walk of life you are in. You can't give up. I don't think about being old. It doesn't concern me at all. I just carry on, you know. It is a matter of staying interested and being vital. It is an attitude. Also, I think that you are lucky if you have a happy family who will appreciate what you have done for them. You are getting paid in lots of other ways.

My father died when he was forty-seven with heart problems. My mother lived until she was eighty-one and she was as sharp as a tack. I was the youngest and she and Betty got on very well together. Mum was on her own so we made her sell her house and come live with us, and she had a very happy last few years because she loved the horses.

My motto in life has been, 'The future belongs to those who plan for it.' When Betty and I celebrated fifty years of marriage, our daughters organised the gift of a magnificent 'hanging' that features this motto. It has pride-of-place in the entrance hallway.

I've tried to set up the children so that they will have a good start, and we help the grandchildren a lot. My planning of late has really been family oriented, you know. It is just one of those things. Most of the good things in life have happened to us. Our life now really revolves around our family. I suppose that we've achieved most of the things in my business. We won forty-one prize premierships, won the Melbourne Cup a couple of times, big races. Now I just enjoy helping the family along their way. I have fulfilled most of my ambitions, put it that way, and I'm lucky, as I'm at peace with the world.

FROM THE UN-HERITAGE LISTED VERANDAH

Max Fatchen

His verse and novels for children are read worldwide. His column, published each Saturday in the *Advertiser*, is read by thousands of people. His name is Max Fatchen, and he is a South Australian icon. As Max's biography, *Other Times*, tells, his adventure with words began in childhood when he entertained neighbours and family with renditions of his poetry. He chose journalism as his career, first with the *News*, and then with the *Advertiser*, where he later became literary editor. As a journalist, Max travelled Australia and sometimes the world, gathering stories. Serendipitously, Max was in Dallas the day JF Kennedy was assassinated. However, it is Max's humorous and poignant observations of life in the suburbs, with rural links, that have particularly captivated and entertained the South Australian public. Whilst seated on his 'un-heritage listed verandah', his reflections on life and people are still fresh, and his writing is eagerly sought by publishers. Max and words are inseparable.

We spoke to Max in his Smithfield home amongst many comfortable chairs ready for entertaining large groups of family and friends. But Max's frequent mirth made his perched position risky!

I don't think anybody should shut themselves in a castle of despair, surrounded by a moat of misery, and pull up all the drawbridges of communication. I know that this happens to people. That's why Jean and I think that it's so important to remain in your own home, among your own things, doing your own thing, because a house is a living entity, especially for elderly people.

I mean, everywhere you go in your home there is a living memory. Memories don't lie in scrapbooks, but are in your mind to be constantly reactivated. If you go to your bath-room, suddenly the bathroom can become people – your children, chubby bodies, soap in their eyes, cries of, 'Where's the towel?' I like to go to the bookshelf and run my hands over the books that have had a significant part in Jean's and my life. They are still there, we are re-reading them, and they are part of our present life. Therefore, in your home, you are living in the past, but also you are, in a sense, in the present that you create for yourself.

Certainly the past is past, and people say, 'Let go of the past,' but the past won't let you go, and that's particularly so for a writer. Writing is a re-creation and a recreation. What I'm saying is that, when I sit down to write, I have a feeling of agelessness, and this gives me the incentive to create. I may not take a walk down the road to Smithfield as far as I should each day, but every morning I take a walk in my mind. When you write, you are, in effect, suddenly in a very lively and diverse world that is your own creation, and which is tapped from the computer of life and experience. Although you're in the present day, the last decade, or whatever you're in, you're also not relinquishing your control of life, or control of yourself, but you are, in a sense, enriching it. A lot of this enrichment comes from the people who read your writing and who write to you.

Well, my main activity is writing. Writing is a continuing adventure.

The purpose of a writer is to reach as many people as possible, but to know the restrictions. You create an identity of incident, and out there you spread your net of words to capture the people who have experienced the incident. For instance, you write something about a horse trough and, from some dusty little town, someone writes because they remember a horse trough. You write about being in the sleep-out when you were young, and suddenly a whole band of letters come in from people who experienced the same. Some of my most interesting mail comes from women between seventy and ninety. So therefore, as you sit in your desk, even though you are elderly, in a sense you have agelessness and timelessness.

There is a two-fold thing to this because I am a children's writer and poet too. So I'm transmitting on two wavelengths. There are elderly people, with whom I identify, and I'm also feeding into the different wavelength of young people. The poetry for children is now published all over the English speaking world, in a hundred and twenty anthologies. I didn't start writing for children until I was well into my forties, and the most productive period of my poetical work has been since retirement. Fortunately, I've kept in contact with children because Jean's taught at virtually every school around here, and we've had generation after generation pass through our house, like young mothers who were her pupils, and who now have their own children.

The thing about children is that they don't believe in this, 'You're up here and I'm down here' stuff. They have a marvellous sense of equality, and they'll write in and tell you if they don't approve of you. One child, a girl about ten years old, wrote in and said, 'Dear Mr Fatchen, I quite liked your last book, but you can do much better!' And she gave me chapter and verse of where I went wrong, which was practically everywhere. She finished up by saying, 'You're quite promising!'

So, my attitude in life is to be 'quite promising'. My philosophy, to an extent, is that I'm still on the journey. The voyage of discovery is going on, and it doesn't end.

Probably psychiatrists would throw up their hands in horror (they always do when they think of me anyway), but my theory is that childhood comes with you; it's inside of you. The child is still there, perhaps covered over with layers of experience, layers of time, inability, illness, and heartbreak in the case of some people, but the child is somewhere there, like the kernel in a nut. Then, when you are older, that child suddenly gives a 'squawk', and comes out. So, that goes into the skill, as an older person, of writing light-hearted poetry for children, and the skills gained from experience contribute to doing intricate verse forms.

I'm very lucky to have a mind that's still resilient. I have four poetry books on the go at the moment, as publishers still come after me, which is wonderful. The requests haven't diminished from the outside world, they've increased! The other day a publisher said, 'We want you to write a children's poem of a thousand words, and we want it on a slightly grotty subject because kids like dirt and rubbish, and all that anti-parent thing.'

You've seen those cranes that have a magnetic thing attached to them, which is lowered down, and when they pull it up there's a great heap of junk hanging on it? Well, I've got that kind of crane in my mind! It goes into the junkyard, and when it does grip onto something, I become terribly vague. Anyway, I sat down in my vagueness and wrote the requested poem in about four days. I wanted to see if I could do it, you know, at this age of seventy-eight. It was sent by fax to the publisher in Sydney at nine o'clock in the morning, and they'd accepted it by eleven.

My family dragged me kicking and screaming into the twentieth century when they gave me a fax machine recently. Now at the *Advertiser* they say, 'I've just had a Max Fax!' Everybody else has got a word processor, but I don't like computers. The other day I got a wonderful letter from someone well into their eighties, who has a computer, and who said, 'I'm surprised you're so backward!' Well, I use my typewriter.

Anyhow, the point I was making before is that as a writer, even at this age, I maintain 'creative tension'. This comes from journalism where you are running for deadlines. The best story in the world is the worst story if you miss the edition, and therefore my mind is constantly filled with edition times. Creative tension, which has a big effect on my life as an elderly person, leads me to be totally involved and immersed in the topic about which I'm writing.

I reached a point when I stopped writing my column in the *Advertiser*. Then, when I was seventy-six, I won a Walkley Award, which is a top award for journalism. So the very able young features editor said, 'What about restarting your column?' It's very interesting how a modern newspaper full of young and brilliant people is kind enough to accept me, and how also some young people ring me for advice.

These days my newspaper writing has become more retrospective because I know that out there is an ageing population, amongst whom are probably some of the most intense readers in the state. Reading is their refuge and their help. So many of them are erudite. They come from an age when the classics were taught at school. Therefore, there is this great pool of elderly people who are looking for a sense of identity. Many people who write to me are widowed, and as I said, they don't want to be locked up in the castle. They want to have the drawbridges down, and to be communicating.

It seems to be that they look back on their life, and often they are wistful. They write about parents who have gone, times that have gone, little towns that have faded, country stores that have closed. What amazes me with elderly people is their minute perception of detail. They become forgetful in other ways, but their minds are particularly focused on certain things. When they write to me about a country store, they describe the colour of the lollies in the jar! They remember detail. They are, in a sense, very focused on the past that I've tried to bring alive in my writing.

They say things like, 'I've read your column for years,' or, 'It's lovely to read about things of which I know.' It's as if they are a bit lonely, and feeling that the great whirlwind of life has gone on, and they're just sitting there. Then suddenly there comes this little 'gong' that awakens them. I have a theory about this.

In my pieces, I write about my 'un-heritage listed veranda', which amuses people immensely. This is where I sit and observe life and all the goings on, but behind this is a very serious theory. When I was a reporter, I interviewed a famous psychiatrist who told me, 'Everybody, if possible, must have a little oasis every day, and in that oasis, have a sense of inner solitude.' You might remember Wordsworth's poem, 'The Daffodils', and where the poem states, 'It flashes on the inward eye, which is the bliss of solitude.'

Now, this inward eye is something that older people particularly have. They may not think it's the 'bliss of solitude', but solitude is a bliss, and solitude is a gathering time. It can be retrospective. It can be introspective. So, I write about my 'un-heritage listed verandah' upon which I sit when the weather's appropriate. This time of solitude, this time of intro-spection, is also where one draws strength. When I say 'oasis', it is a pool of reassurance, I suppose, where you go and take a drink. This is what I find fortifies me at my age.

I'll frankly admit, you know, that I'm a coward in some things. I don't make any profound pronouncements about the hereafter. The 'nowafter' is my thing. I'm fortunate to have come so far, but life itself is a series of stages.

Spirituality comes from all around me, not so much from within. People say things like, 'I've had an awakening, a great revelation.' I don't decry that, but my revelations are the ordi-nary people around me, in all kinds of situations, and some-times in the great tragedies of the world. These people, including the elderly people who've lost everything, have enriched me because of their dauntless human spirit. I draw my spirituality from contact with people not in the public eye, who are not wealthy, and who in many cases are isolated, down-cast, down-beaten, and suddenly the beacon comes on, the light-house is lit, and the coast is clear.

Especially with the elderly people I've encountered, there is some kind of reinforcement, some kind of spiritual con-crete in their feats of endurance. The waves are beating over them, the inevitability of life and death, and while their hold on life may be slipping, their hold on some of the realities, some of the wonderful experiences, some of the strengths of character, doesn't slip. Spirituality comes from children too, because they write in to me, or come and talk to me, and are quite uninhibited. So therefore, I feel that if you want to be spiritual, although it's good to have a belief in the tenets of Christianity, and spirituality is hopefully a thing of the future too, it is really a thing of the present, because it arises from people themselves.

Some years ago, on separate occasions, I had the privilege of sitting down with Aboriginal elders. Well, one of the things I've learnt from them was the wisdom in the bush, the environment. This learning had a spiritual quality. I learnt that these are very spiritual people – the Dreaming of their people, and the legends. It was very impressionable, sitting there in the bush with the stars out and all that.

This affected me, you know. To me there were links with my life as a child on a farm on the Adelaide Plains. Getting back to the verandah syndrome, my father would say, 'Come out and look at the sky, mate.' He would give me lessons about clouds, because farmers are good forecasters. I mean, here we have all the weather satellites going overhead and streaming down information, but you get a wise old farmer, and he can give the satellites a bit of a run for their money. As we looked at the clouds, my father would also teach me the beauty of the sky, the beauty of itself, a changing character.

Both Jean and I still do this. Jean will say, 'Come out and look at the stars and the moon.' You face the great mystery when you go outside, and one of the important things to me, as an older person, is that I still like an element of mystery in my life. I don't want everything explained to me. I mean, the scientist has got a theory. Politicians have got a theory why the economy's gone this way, or why the yen's gone down. I know these things are important, but when I sit on my verandah in the afternoon on a cool winter's day, and those clouds begin marching across the sky, I think that this is having a little glimpse at immortality. There I come back to the wisdom of the environment that these older Aboriginal men taught me.

They talked about other things also. When I sat down

with the old men at Yalata, one of them talked of 'Old Mr Eyre'. 'Old Mr Eyre so-and-so.' Suddenly I realised they were talking about Edward John Eyre, the explorer. It had come down in their story-telling. The other Aboriginal man that I sat down with was in Arnhem Land, and he was one of their 'song men'. They are the poets of their people!

They had a great effect on my life and on my philosophy now as an elderly person. I realise that life has a vibrancy no matter how old you are. So, you want to be totally involved, to have a lively mind, communicate with people, talk to people around you. You remember John Donne's words, 'No man is an island.' Society shouldn't let older people be an island, as the responsibility is not only theirs, but it's the people's around them. That gets back to the fact that it's so important to stay in your own home if you can, surrounded by the neighbours you know, have children calling on the door (even if they do eat all your iceblocks), and to not think of the community as some distant city.

It's lovely to have a marriage that's lasted fifty-six, nearly fifty-seven years. It's been wonderful being married to someone who's highly intelligent, with an interest in poetry, and who is a literary person. Jean writes very well. She writes an enormous number of letters, to everybody, everywhere. Nobody's birthday is forgotten. Jean's been one of my great strengths, you know. With Jean, life is like going in to bat having Don Bradman at one end, and I'm at the other!

One night I had a telephone call, and there's a beautiful voice on the other end of the phone, a young girl's voice, I'd say about eleven, twelve. She said, 'My name's Katie, and I'm going to recite one of your poems in a drama performance, and I'd like to know all about you.' 'Right Katie,' so the great man gives all the usual kind of stuff! Jean is always very aware, and after this has gone on for some time, she called out, 'Cut it short, because if that child's on long-distance, there'd be a real problem for her parents!' So we terminated our conversation, and before we did, I asked, 'Where are you ringing from Katie?' She said, 'I'm ringing from London.'

Anyway, a couple of days later the telephone rang again. This time it was an American voice, a man, 'I'm Katie's father,' he said. I thought, 'Oh!!' because we had this image of Katie's parents begging by the roadside to pay for the telephone call. I said, 'I'm terribly sorry for the length of that call, as I know it must have cost a lot of money,' blab, blab, blab. 'Oh,' he said, 'I'm not worried about that. Katie's mislaid your address and she just wants it, you see.' And he said, 'Don't worry about me, as I'm one of the heads of the World Bank!'

Family's tremendously important, I think. We have two sons, a daughter, and six grandchildren. We have one great-grandchild, Molly, and another great-grandchild on the way. They're all very affectionate and they all keep in touch. Jean can take a lot of the credit for that. They all do different things, and they're sparkling individuals. I had a remarkable mother, and a marvellously kind and gentle father.

One of my books, coming out soon, I've dedicated to Molly. I usually dedicate my books to children, and one or two have been dedicated to dogs. That goes down very well, although I don't know what the dogs thought!

And there is the outer family, which are your readers. For me, it is important to touch a tiny part of as many lives as I can, and to give them a sense of hope and justification for their own existence. The human race is a family, although sadly it doesn't look like it half the time. I was in the second world war, but it wasn't a frontline position, as I was in the airforce ground staff, in communications.

Age has a wisdom that comes from experience, or hurt, or joy, or anything else, because you are looking back on the chronicles of time. I think that wisdom is refined with age, but people generally have wisdom for their age and their time and their experience, and if they put it all together, they may make some sense of it. Life's a highway. It's got a lot of parking bays and it's a good idea to pull off the road and watch the traffic. That's what I mean about having an oasis.

I remember the older people from my childhood, like my grandmother, Sophia, out on the farm. I remember her in her pinny, and later, with her walking stick. On farms then, you only had pretty primitive implements. Life was difficult. There was no money, and you went through the Depression by the skin of your teeth. I see the vision of Sophia's patience and her face, and somehow she's come through life for me. That infinite patience and acceptance – I think that's something!

And then there was my Grandfather Ridgway, who'd been a farmer, and who lived at Tennyson. He took me walking in the swamps that became West Lakes, and he understood nature. There again is that wisdom of the environment. He was the first one to teach me about that, and you don't forget these things.

The songs Henry Krips and I wrote for the Birdsville Track have become very popular – I wrote the words. When you're out there at night, sitting on the Track, you have the feeling that the land is prowling around just outside the firelight. You get this feeling that it's there watching you and assessing you, as it's done for thousands of years for other people, of other colours, and other kinds. One of these songs captures the feeling of the old men with the wisdom of environment, and captures the enormous effect that nature has on me.

I've been in the outback. I've seen nature at it's angriest, like the 1956 River Murray floods, and the sea particularly. You'll find the sea and the river right throughout my work. I'll never forget a particular experience I had on the river years ago, which is described in my biography. It triggered my whole writing career. And that's where the mystery comes in to it. What great power was moving then?

For many men, they are drawn to the land for their form of work, or they go out in it to get away from their work. It's a kind of hospital of the mind for many; you go out to be cured of things, and although you may not be totally cured, you're put into remission from the attacks of life. Women are conscious of these things too, but I think men are inclined to seek the land because they are looking for something that will ease their lot, in a sense. The land can be, in effect, a kind of ointment that you rub on the wounds of time.

Jean and I like travelling, although we don't travel as much as we used to. I like fishing. I go to catch fish, certainly, but I go to sit on a jetty and be at one with the sea because this is where so much of my inspiration has come from, especially around Port Victoria and the Gulf. Here again is the spirituality bit, because the sea's a very spiritual place for me. It's not just the fishing line and the bait and where the mullet are biting, it's something deeper. Much of my best poetry and best writing has come from the sea.

We rise reasonably early. Over a usual day, the first two or three hours are devoted to writing, either revising, or looking at things. The point about writing is that it's an all day thing. I don't mean physically doing it all day, but all the time you're looking out for ideas. When I do write, I can write quickly, compose quickly – it's my newspaper training.

Also Jean and I read quite a bit. Jean reads a diversity of books, and I love reading poetry. Writers reach you out of other centuries, don't they? Biblical writers reach you from eons ago. And the old Aboriginal legends come from thousands of years back, so therefore the whole thing is a great continuing process.

I was surprised and delighted that on Christmas Day, an American cable television show, with an audience of sixty-eight million people, included a reading of one of my poems. There again, this is the business of outreach, because as writers, you never know how far your writing reaches out into the world. You never know whether there's some child or older person out there, where your writing has wakened an echo, or given just a little bit of strength; someone else out there's had that kind of experience, somebody out there understands, and they've reached out and touched me. And that's the ultimate thing in writing.

Words are our lifeline. They can sparkle, or they can thunder, or they can hurt, or they can inspire. Therefore, for older people, regarding the art of language and speech, it's important to talk to them, and to keep this kind of interchange fresh. I think old people can have a lot to say, but often they've got nobody to listen. One of the greatest arts of writing is listening. You don't talk all the time. You listen and watch and interpret, that's what you do.

I love words and I love food! Now, my young GP is marvellous. We have been fortunate to have a wonderful series of GPs nearby in Gawler. But in regard to my eating, my present GP, he's shaking his head so much he's got vertigo!

Regarding food, I love all the wicked things, but I don't like wine, and I'm teetotaller – more or less lifelong. And I've never smoked cigarettes. I had a brief session with cigars, but other people evacuated the jetty, so I thought I better stop! But I've always loved food. I've been a great pasty lover, pie lover, and definitely a cream bun lover. Especially those fabulous creamy 'kitchener buns'!

This love of food comes from those country days when everybody did their own cooking, and when the baker came in a cart and delivered his bread. We received great enjoyment out of food. Sunday tea in the country was an almost religious kind of festival. If you were asked to tea, the people who asked you made sure there were cream cakes, magnificent jellies, and trifles for which you'd kill. There were sponge cakes that you could lie on like a mattress. Of course, people prided themselves on their cooking, and at those country shows, you know, the sponge cake rivalry was ferocious. Like it was the Melbourne Cup!

Jean's a marvellous cook. For years, until we got a bit too old for it, we had a turkey day here where we invited all our friends from writing, and everywhere else, and they'd all come, and Jean would cater for it.

So I'm overweight and I need to use a stick. It's a worry that a lot of elderly people, because of their pride, won't use walking sticks. I'll tell you how I learnt a lesson about this, and it involves food too!

I didn't have my walking stick, and I was going to see my mother who was in hospital down at Western Community Hospital. I was walking along Currie Street, and the pavement was uneven where they were doing some building. Here I was, you know, a great, big, hefty, overweight person, and I came a terrible cropper! I tripped over, and all the younger people around rushed to my assistance, which was very sweet of them because I hurt myself – I skinned my elbow, and winded myself! Well, they lifted me to my feet, people were brushing me down, young women were fussing over me, and I said, 'Look, I'll be alright now,' because they did fix me up,

I must admit. But one young man hovered around still, and I said, 'There's no need to wait, as I'm quite alright.' And he asked, 'Please could I have back my finger bun?' When I fell, I made a terrible grab at him, and I must have grabbed his finger bun, and held it in this deathly clutch. I gave it back to him, but it was so mashed up, he probably had to eat the paper too!

So that's walking sticks, and I use them now. My thing is, never mind about pride, think about comfort and wellbeing, you know. There can, of course, be something regal about a walking stick. Max Harris had one, and Oscar Wilde always carried a walking stick!

What is not good about ageing is the inevitability of the lifespan. I suppose, to a degree, it's also the lack of mobility, if that prevents you doing the things you want to do, but I've never been very mobile anyway, so that doesn't worry me. I've never been a very lively, physical person, and I've never excelled greatly at any of the sports, although I do like to walk.

For some, I suppose being older is not good because of poor health, but talking generally about older people, I think the worst thing is to be lonely and ignored and put aside. I mean, the deprivation of company, or caring, or people, or that drawbridge of communication that I spoke about earlier, where nobody thinks that you've got anything worthwhile to say. The important thing is that everybody's got something worthwhile to say. They just need to be encouraged, and to be shown that their life has importance, meaning and relevance, not only just for themselves, but also perhaps for other people.

Sometimes, if you can bring two people together, they can exchange some of these fears and triumphs and everything else, and in the end, in a kind of contract, they can build up their own resources, and their own self again. As an older person, you should not feel diminished, because you are a human being, and whatever has overtaken your life, you have something to say, and something to give, and something that's worth listening to.

Alternatively, I think the best thing about being older, as far as I'm concerned, and I'm talking as a writer, is that you have an oversight of your whole life. Therefore, it's like standing on a hill, and the city's laid out before you, and you're lucky enough, perhaps capable enough, of looking at it, assessing it, sitting down and evaluating it, and eventually reliving it.

> *'So much to tell,' the old man said,*
> *'Before you make your dancing rhyme'*
> *Recalling busy years that fled*
> *Along the corridors of time.*
>
> *'What's gone? What's left? What's there to say?*
> *Will memory's gate swing slowly shut*
> *And close upon my yesterday?'*
> *My plaintive cry . . . if only . . . but . . . ?*
>
> *So I'll not bore you with my schemes*
> *But simply this small thought repeat . . .*
> *The cool oasis of my dreams*
> *Still has its healing waters sweet.*

Max Fatchen, 1999

MIMILI, MY PLACE

tjilpi Kantji

In the far north of South Australia, just south of the Northern Territory border, and on the edge of the Great Victorian Desert, *tjilpi* Kantji lives at a place called Mimili. An Aboriginal community of about one hundred persons, Mimili is on Pitjantjatjara land. An entry permit is required in order to travel into this area and for visiting any of the Aboriginal communities scattered around the land. The title *'tjilpi'* means 'old man who is initiated', and Kantji is a greatly respected elder of his tribe. His son, Shannon, is chairperson of the Mimili community. Sometimes *tjilpi* Kantji travels to 'sit down' with others, such as the old people at Indulkana, another Aboriginal community about sixty kilometres to the east of Mimili. On these visits he rolls out his swag at one of the nearby camps, perhaps down near the creek, and sleeps under the stars. Over the years, *tjilpi* Kantji has been a hunter, station-hand, stockman, minder of camels, and also an opal miner.

Tjilpi Kantji sat on the corner of a pin-striped mattress in the shade beside his son's house as he spoke to us through an interpreter.

I'm *Wati*. This mean initiated man. I was born beyond the hill next here to Mimili. Now that place called 'Bakers Well'. Seventy kilometres that way, perhaps. Born long time back. Don't know when.

When little, bush tucker good. The wild figs, we call'em *ili*. The quandongs are *mangata*. Good tucker, same as what we get feed'em white fella. Same thing bush tucker. We pick'em up from ground. We eat'em quick one, you know. See them longa ground, pick'em up, eat'em, then go along. Know what to eat'em – Mum tell me.

Brothers and sisters, all gone now. Muntji, William, Tilly. Maybe some older than me. My sister Muntji older. All gone heaven now, and I'm behind. The only one left.

All born before white fella come – just one white fella then. That same white fella here long time – Mickey Daddo. Built house with stone. We been see'em new house built here at Mimilli. My Uncle here then. We don't know build stone, you know. Can't read properly like white fella. That house now long gone. This then cattle station – called 'Granite Downs'.

Before this, all old people's land. No horses. No cattle. Nothing. Old people's land, this one. Aboriginal people. Always. Good land, but not always.

Young man, we spear'em rabbits and *kanyala*, that kangaroo. Euros too. Euros were up in those hills there, near here. Always there. Kangaroo on the *manta*, the flat ground.

When I live at Watjitjata, the old men, then like I am now, it was okay for them to sit. Sometimes they would stay. Some days they go out for meat. For rabbits, not kangaroo. The old people, sometimes they go for hunting. Sometimes old people still catch'em.

Old people looked after the land. Lots of rock-holes.

They were all dug around, cleaned out, and left. Then, after it rained, we could go stay there. Would go rockhole, and sit down, and the young fellas were learning from the *tjilpi* – the old men. Also, teach'em how to catch'em kangaroo. Other places, always sit down with old people.

My father a good hunter. He would go to Witjintji. He would take me there. We would go together. He would dig for rabbits, and kill'em. Lots of rabbits, from the burrows. He was a truly good man.

When young, that time, we went away, and we arrived at Murul. Then, from Murul we went on. There no road, and we see camels. First time. We think it was evil spirit! I think this too. Then come Harold Brumby – white fella there with camel.

Then, long ago, I travelled with camels to Pipalyatjara. Helped the white fella Brumby. There were altogether twelve camels. That white fella was thinking of sending them to Mount Davies – for the dogs. We catch'em dingoes, for the scalps. We got rations and money for the scalps. The camels were carrying a lot of tucker. Twelve camels – each one four camel-bags. A lot of flour.

One time, I live at Coober Pedy. Once, I think. There for a fair while, opal mining. Tried, but couldn't find it. Not much money.

And *wati*, initiated man, he might look about for kangaroo. Some people go away, you know, for hunting. Might shoot'em, if he got rifle. We got'em with a spear long time before white fella. We go from here, go along hill there. Euro went down longa hill there. He come down this way too, front of there.

Been catch'em kangaroo. Bring'em back here and make'em trench. Chuck'em on fire, then cover'em up. Pull'em out, and clean'em out. Any part good, but no salt! Salt with rabbits, but no salt with kangaroo. White fella cut tail off kangaroo, but we got'em that one too.

I make'em spear. All old men make'em. All of them. I get'em from top of hill. I been cut'em down. Long one, straight one, like a piece of pipe. Cut'em right down the bottom. If you want'em, we go from here for climb that hill. Only, not now. I'm weak. Old men's spirits are get'em weak. My spear, I been give it to grandson. He's over there, lying down. I don't teach'em how to make spear – that long time ago. That's why I got'em now.

I learn make spear from my father and grandfather. They take'em show me behind that hill, behind there. Before, we got'em sort of stone, same as the chisel. A little bit hard now! We got'em now – chisels. We got little tomahawk, you know.

We can camp outside, on the ground. Sleep outside. Not sleep when inside house. I sleep'em longa ground. Make'em little bit of trench. Put'em up a windbreak. So, a fire, on two sides. Put head on ground. We put'em no pillow. Before, no swag. Now, a swag.

I sit here, with my son, Shannon. No other children, except for Yami Lester. He my step-son. Shannon got five children. Boys and girls. One girl in wheelchair – she born like that. Can't move her legs. Shannon got one grandchild. Sometime, I talk with them. Tell them stories here. Boys and girls.

Mimili alright. My place this one. Can't go another place. All the time Mimili. My place, that's why I'm here. Own the land and own the place. Lot of white fella mob go in, ask questions. This our business. They not happy that way. Say, 'Get out!' This is people's country. We sit down. White men don't know anything about before. Black fella different. White man feed by himself, for himself. That's why all this young fella now, they drink wine. That's why they get'em weak.

I've got a Dreaming. If a white fella ask me that, I can't tell him. Only tell young man – talking sacred. Some older people do that. Let'em know. I hear'em about Christian God. Hear in church. They teach me. They still come here. Have'em sacred business as well. Got a Dreaming.

Sometime, I walk'em around, you know. Make'em me happy. Go sit down at Indulkana. I like'em sit down there. Only when cold there. Not the hot time. Also, sometime I go past the hill, other direction. Not walk far now. Not now – finish, my legs! Just only close. Got'em me cough too.

And somebody, I want'em, might be, carry me round with car. Long way. Then I sit down. Talk. Sit down with somebody. Have a good yarn. That's what I like, you know. Might go with someone. Might go alonga bush. Might chuck anything in. Might shoot *malu* – kangaroo. Come back. Might have good feed.

Same like white fella, we get'em old. Everyone get'em old. Can't be a young fella all day, all the time. It's enough. Might get'em old. Might die any day. We can't see time, you know. My son might finish his time yet, you know. Some live short time. Some live long time. It happens. Can't help me – been big long time. That's the way.

The young people, they look after old people. Always, the young people of the family. We care for our own fathers. Grandsons look after grandparents. When they getting old, they sit down, and young people help'em. Care for'em. Son or daughter may bring'em water. Cook'em tucker. Bring'em food. And love'em. Also, too far to get'em *kapi* – water. Can't walk. That's why we like young women look after you. Get'em *kapi*, you know.

When they get'em proper old, they get'em weak, and young fellas make fire for'em. Love'em.

THE FULL VINTAGE

Peter Lehmann

Peter Lehmann has made fine wine in the Barossa Valley of South Australia since 1947. As a fifth-generation Barossan, and with a strong sense of 'doing what is right', his loyalty to the local grape growers is renowned. Both his name and his persona are considered by many to be synonymous with the Barossa. The winemaking team at Peter Lehmann Wines Limited has produced wines that have won numerous prestigious awards nationally, including the Royal Melbourne Show's Jimmy Watson Trophy, and at the international level, trophies at the International Wine and Spirit Competition. A risk-taker, who has ensured that the company has survived several challenges, his chosen logo for the winery is the Queen of Clubs, the gambler's card. Peter was awarded membership of the Order of Australia in 1975, which was the inaugural list of that award. Other major activities and contributions have included wine judging, patron and ambassador for various clubs, presidency of the Barossa Vintage Festival, and being president of several Barossa sporting organisations.

We sat around Peter's kitchen table during the interview, his huge German Shepherd lying at his feet, the phone ringing often and people drifting in and out.

I've stepped back a bit from the business, but I still do a complete vintage. During the rest of the year, I'm sort of involved in the tasting game, classifying the wines for whichever label they go into. For instance, when we make shiraz, we might make up to forty different tanks of shiraz. Some are almost predestined in the sense that we know in which direction they are going, but that has to be checked and the wine classified organoleptically for smell, taste and appearance.

This year will be my fifty-second vintage. The time's got to come when I will retire, but I'll still be sticky-beaking around. When I was talking about retiring a little while ago, the powers that be, that is my fellow directors and my wife Margaret, suggested that would be a very foolish thing to do. Probably I will only completely retire when they put me in a box! Obviously, I'm the founder of the company and I'll always have more than a passing interest, but how much longer I'll be doing the full vintage, I don't know.

We make wines to a style that is, as I say, almost preordained in direction, and that applies to all the different styles we make. Winemaking is something like nursing little babies, their whole future is determined in the first two or three weeks of their life, while they're fermenting, so tender loving care is needed when looking after the wines.

A good solid day's tasting in the tasting laboratory can create enough work in the cellar for up to two or three months, but I'm not as involved as I used to be in the earlier days. We have six winemakers, including my eldest son and me in a 'non-hands-on' situation. So, four winemakers are actively monitoring, watching. I suppose that my knowledge of winemaking influences the product through the training of the people involved. Our chief winemaker, Andrew Wigan, and I have been together for about twenty-six years.

When there's a wine in question, usually the majority of us will say that it should go one way or the other. It's fairly hard to explain, but say you've got twenty different shiraz, then invariably three or four of us will select three top wines. Now, I might have them in one order, and Andrew might have them in another order, and someone else in another order, but the top three Shiraz will be consistent. The majority wins. I've got the power of veto but I've never had to exercise it.

Once you delegate, you've got to step back, otherwise they'll say, 'Well, I'm going somewhere else.' I mean, I was in a situation where I wanted to be part of a particular wine's destiny without interference from those up top, so I realised very quickly when I appointed Andrew chief winemaker that I had to delegate, and let him do his thing. Maybe one of my greatest successes has been my ability to delegate. If things had gone badly, then obviously I would've stepped in and taken corrective measures, but it hasn't been necessary. We work as a team. Almost a family really!

When I say 'a family', this includes the growers. We do get on very well together, and I've been dealing with them for forty-plus years. If not them, then their families, as a lot of the dads have 'fallen off the perch'. I remember a particular grower, who is now a mature man, probably in his mid-forties, as a little kid being dragged in by his father. Now, in turn, this fellow is bringing his son to 'learn the ropes'.

It's terrific to see the young fellows still taking an interest in grape growing because I think the Barossa Valley is special in the sense that the majority of the growers see themselves as caretakers of the soil for future generations. This, of course, is not unlike the way Aboriginal people look at the land. The growers here see their role in life as handing the land on to their children in better shape than when they received it. I've never seen the Barossa looking better, there is a terrific amount of pride in the place. It's very exciting. Also, grape prices have been very good lately.

I really enjoy the vintage and I like meeting the people. I still love doing vintage, it's a very exciting period of time. I've always done my winemaking from the weighbridge, so you're in constant contact with your growers. We always have a few sticks of metwurst hanging on the back of the door, and there are usually pickled sour cucumbers and pickled onions to share while you're assessing the grapes, weighing them, chatting with the growers.

Also, we do most of our vintage entertainment in the form of weighbridge lunches, meeting a lot of interesting people. People drop in. When we're entertaining, it's usually ham and there's always cheese. It's just a nice relaxed way. That's how we've always done it.

In the off-season, which is any time other than vintage, I still do a little bit of promotional work interstate. I've given up wine judging, but I still do an occasional guest appearance such as two last year at the Sheraton in Perth and also up in Brisbane. In Perth it was their twentieth anniversary and they wanted a couple of the oldies to come back, so I did. We also still do the odd promotional trip, lunch for the press, or we might have wine dinners introducing a new label.

I've been a winemaker ever since I left school in 1947. In today's terminology, you'd have to say I was a 'drop-out'. In other words, I would have taken any job in the world to get out of school. As luck would have it, Mum was at a party in Angaston, and the then secretary of Yalumba, a bloke called Alf Wark, just happened to mention that they were looking for a likely lad to train under their winemaker Rudy Kronberger.

I don't know if I would have described myself as a 'likely lad', however!

At that time I was home for the weekend. I had gone to Immanuel College for three years, but during the third year there, my Dad died. The following year I went to Nuriootpa High School, but as my older brother had gone to Prince Alfred College, Mum thought that it was only fair that I got a chance to go to a non-Lutheran school, just for the experience. Prince's were full up at the time, so I was able to go to Scotch College.

Anyhow, I was home for the weekend from Scotch, and Mum mentioned that Yalumba was looking for a lad. I 'wagged' the Monday, got on my treddley, and went for an interview with Mr Wark at 5 pm. I got the job.

I was almost seventeen when I started. That's how I came to do my apprenticeship at Yalumba, and I was there for twelve years, but it would have been a good ten years before I was actually put in charge of an operation. Then Saltram advertised for a winemaker-manager, for which I applied and was successful. So I left Yalumba to be with Saltram for twenty years. Those days, apart from the fact that most wine was fortified, it was also rationed. It was actually scarce, and consequently grapes were very hard to come by. Part of my job at Saltram, apart from winemaking, was also to try and increase the tonnage.

Well, I'm Barossa born and bred. In fact, I'm fifth-generation Barossa. Being a local lad, gradually I cajoled and enticed a few more growers, year by year. The fact that I was the son of the late Pastor Lehmann didn't do me any harm either! When I started at Saltram, there was only about a five hundred ton crush. By 1977, we were close to five thousand ton.

At that time, things began to get very traumatic, and I

thought the end of the world had come. Firstly, the pastoral company Dalgetty, which then owned Saltram, made a decision in London that they weren't going to buy any grapes from the contract grape growers for the 1978 vintage. I fought every way I possibly could to get them to change their mind, but they wouldn't.

They allowed me to form an outside company, which was the beginning of Peter Lehmann Wines. We actually did two vintages where we bought the fruit from the growers and flogged it off to the trade. Actually, it worked very well, and then Dalgetty sold to Seagram, and Seagram made it clear that I would not be able to continue the process. So I resigned and found a couple of partners and built this winery. In 1980 we had our first vintage, and now we're coming up to our twentieth.

It wasn't that one day I sat down and said, 'Well, now I'm going to build a winery,' it was sort of forced on me in order to protect the livelihood of the growers. It was a big step and I tell you that it nearly drove me around the bend. I must say though that Margaret was an absolute, terrific help. I couldn't have done it without her. Also, I had good friends.

Starting my own winery brought about a complete change in my life. Whilst still at Saltram, I had bought a property up the other side of Angaston, which was going to be where we'd live when I retired, but that fell by the board with the new winery venture.

Things were going along here quite swimmingly, until our original terrific partners (who were also an English company) were having a few take-over squabbles and needed a bit more money. That started off a chain of events until, in 1992, we looked like being dismembered and sold off bit by bit.

That's when I made my move and bought the company,

cashing in my superannuation to run the 1993 vintage because the old company couldn't. I still had the shelf companies from when I ran the two vintages at Saltram. I'd kept the licences alive, so I dusted one of those off, and did the vintage. Later in that year, we floated successfully, with most growers and all the winery team buying shares. From there we've gone from strength to strength under the leadership of my eldest son, Douglas, who is our managing director. It is wonderful that he is doing such a good job.

I was about fifty-nine by that stage, and it was eight or nine of the most harrowing months we've ever experienced. It was terrible.

I think when you're under stress weak points give out, or something. I've had cancer twice, but, well, I'm still here! In 1970 I had a scare. I thought it must be appendicitis, and the local boys opened me up, decided it was too big for them, and stitched me straight up again. Of course, the word went around: 'Did you hear about Lehmann? They opened him and sewed him straight up again!' A specialist found out that it wasn't cancer in that case. Then, in 1990, I had a cancerous polyp in the bowel, so I had that removed, but somehow my ureter was severed, and that resulted in losing a kidney.

And then, in late 1993, I discovered I had a little cancer in the prostate. Consequently, I was the first in Australia to have the 'seed implant' treatment, which was done in Western Australia. It's worked for me. Ever since I had the treatment my Prostate Specific Antigen has been less than one.

My father died from a coronary at fifty-five, but I seem to have had the good fortune to have inherited my mother's genes. My mother's aged magnificently. She's a very simple person with a very simple life. When my father died, she was widowed and unencumbered, so she looked after her mother,

her father, and her brother, until they died. She's now ninety-six, and up until only a few months ago she was doing her own gardening and everything. Really fit. Then she decided that she'd move into a retirement village. None of us would have been game to suggest it. My local GP, who's very, very good, says to me every time I have a check-up, 'I hope you're still sending your mother flowers!'

When I had the cancer scare that turned out not to be cancer, I thought, 'Oh, my God!' I remember getting all the family together and cooking them a farewell dinner. I cooked roast turkey and got a bit emotional. I think that prepared me for when the actual cancer occurred twenty years later.

I remember being interviewed by Philip Satchell in 1990. That year we'd won the Jimmy Watson Trophy, in my case for the second time, and his producer said, 'Philip would like to talk to you about winning the Jimmy Watson for the second time.' Just before we went on air, Philip asked, 'Oh, do you mind if I just mention your bowel cancer?' And I said, 'No, it's a fact of life, fine.' So the interview went something like, 'Well, Peter, it must be a great thrill winning the Jimmy Watson.' I said, 'Yeah, terrific, Philip.' I was then expecting to go on discussing that, but he said, 'Now, you've had bowel cancer?' Straight into it, and then he asked, 'If my memory serves me right, Peter, you used to smoke.' I said, 'What do you mean *used to*, Philip? I still do.' Horrified, he exclaimed: 'What? You mean you've had cancer and you're still smoking?' I said: 'Philip, I'm not advocating that any of your listeners smoke. I'd advise them not to, but the fact of the matter is that I do smoke, and as far as attributing my particular form of cancer to smoking, I would have had to smoke through my bum!' And he said, 'Peter! You're on ABC radio!'

Occasionally you suddenly come to the realisation that

you are sixty-eight and that's getting fairly old, but you know, I'm mentally about fifteen. However, as the saying goes, 'Getting old is a bugger, except when you consider the alternative!' I do know that inevitably we're all going to die, but I don't dwell on that. I just think, 'Oh well, when you do, you do.' I've taken precautions so Margaret and the kids will be fairly well provided for. When Margaret and I were married, we worked out we would be living on minus twenty bucks a week. Winemakers in those days weren't very well paid, and also there wasn't a great deal of inherited wealth, being the son of a parson.

Although my father was a Lutheran Pastor, I'm not really religious. It may happen one day. I mean, deep down there must be something planted in the first fourteen years of my life before my father died. I think the Sermon on the Mount influences me, and 'do unto others as you would have them do unto you', but the rest I find very hard to come to grips with.

I've got time on my hands now, as I'm not doing day-to-day stuff for the business continually. A couple of mates and I do a lot of off-road driving, in the outback. They reckon they're too old to camp out, so we plan our trips such that we always have a motel or a hotel booked. Last year we went through the Big Desert and the Little Desert. Mostly we've been up north, but together no further than Birdsville.

It's usually five days out bush. Margaret calls us the 'Three Queens of the Desert', *Priscilla*-style! We have a lot of fun. We always have a leisurely lunch out in the scrub, a barbecue, and take it in turns to drive. So the driver doesn't drink, or he might have, you know, one, maybe two glasses, but the others can have a couple of bottles of good red. We had some trips planned for this year, but they've been put on hold now, because sadly one has recently had a stroke.

There have been other trips, as Margaret enjoys them too. Last year, together with some friends, Margaret and I went from near Quorn across to Coober Pedy, and then due west through the Victoria Desert out to Maralinga country (we saw where they let off the two atomic bombs), Emu Junction, Voakes Hill Corner, and then down to Cook and Nullarbor. I love that sort of thing.

When we do interstate trips Margaret is the navigator and I always drive, but one rule is that she has to find a different road to get from point A to point B. So, during a trip up to the Sunshine Coast, we crossed the Great Divide six times, zigzagging. We always allow plenty of time. Maybe two or three times a year we get away like that, for perhaps a week or so at a time.

On one of the trips to Perth, Margaret and I drove up to Katherine and turned left, coming down through the Kimberlies, which I'd always wanted to see. I used to say, 'I won't go overseas again until I've seen the Kimberlies.' Now I'm saying, 'I won't go overseas again until I go through Kakadu, Cape York and down through there.' I'll not have covered all of Australia then, but large portions of it.

I do love driving, and I used to love the Variety Club Bashes, but I think 1988 was my last full-time Bash. My eldest son, Douglas, took over and is now an entrant each year. I'm one of the South Australian ambassadors of the Variety Club, which I'm proud to support.

We still do a reasonable amount of socialising. I don't know if everyone's the same, but it seems that as you get older you tend to become a bit more antisocial. Maybe it's just because you can't be bothered, or perhaps because as you get older most of your friends 'fall off the perch'!

Margaret is incredibly busy at the moment. She is the

original caring person, so you name a committee, and she's either been on it, or is on it. She's now Councillor Lehmann. She stood for the Council a couple of years ago and I said, 'You've got no chance as you're not a Barossan, you've only been here for twenty-seven years.' Well, she topped the poll! She doesn't leave anything to chance, as she's really a very thorough person.

We've been together for thirty years now. Margaret and I have two children, and I have three children from my first marriage. The family is pretty important and we regularly see all of the kids, with the exception of my daughter, who lives in Queensland. The others all live in the Barossa.

I have eight grandchildren, which is terrific. The grand-children all enjoy each other, but I'm not really the clinging sort of person. I just like to be treated as an individual, and I don't go for the 'grandpoppy' bit. All the kids call me Peter. Whenever one of them says, 'Dad', I say, 'How much?' They call me Peter, or Pop, or maybe Dad. It varies, but we've got a very easy, friendly relationship. We're all mates.

Our two closest neighbours are my eldest son, Douglas, and our son David, who lives right next-door in the place up on the hill where Margaret and I lived while we were building our present home. David's ambition is to develop his own little boutique winery. You know, grow and make. I told him, 'The only way to do that is to really understand viticulture, because great wines are made in the vineyard, not the winery.' So currently he's working for the bloke who looks after Margaret's and my vineyards. Up until five or six years ago we didn't own any vineyards, but through the change in fortunes, or circumstances, we do now.

I used to be an avid race-goer but Margaret sort of cured me of that, not because she was disapproving, but she was just absolutely bored. I took her to the races a few times, and she'd take a bag with a book in it, sit in a corner and read while I'd go off to have a bet. I used to own some trotting horses and I do still go to the trots occasionally – I'm the patron of the Kapunda Trotting Club.

I read a fair bit, not the paper very much, usually novels, as I really get engrossed in some crime fiction. I love music. Each year we have the annual 'Barossa Under The Stars' in a natural amphitheatre between our place and Richmond Grove Winery. There's a lovely stretch of grass and they put the stage down by the Para River. We can seat about seven thousand. This year's guest artists are Tony Bennett and Julie Anthony. Julie and her husband will be our house guests.

But that is a different sort of music to the music I love. If you look at our CDs, you'll see it's mostly baroque and beyond. We're very strong supporters of the 'Barossa Music Festival', which I really enjoy – not only the music, but meeting some of the great artists of the world. I'm a Mozart, Beethoven, Schubert, and Vivaldi fan. Switch any radio on, in the car or the house, and it's always on 103.9, ABC FM.

I think that you've got to force yourself to do a certain amount of exercise, which I do through gardening. I still do all the gardens around the house, which is a fairly vast expanse of area. I've toyed with the idea of putting in pop-up sprinklers and everything else, but I think, 'Oh God, my footprints will get more sedentary than ever.' Vegetable growing is enjoyable, so I do that too. If it weren't, I wouldn't do it. I mean, I like growing odd little things. I've even got a large mango tree, although it's only three years old. Also there are avocados fruiting for the first time.

To age well, and this might sound like a sales pitch, but I'm sure that a couple of glasses of red each day does no harm whatsoever. In fact, I think it does a lot of good. Also, there's that eternal search for the right soul mate, and you're lucky if you find a relationship like I have with Margaret. That's one of the best things. Well, she's also my best friend.

Don't take life too seriously. Most importantly, don't take yourself too seriously. Margaret says that I haven't done anything that I haven't wanted to do, and that I've not enjoyed – eventually!

GLOBAL IMPACT

Basil Hetzel

Professor Basil Hetzel AC graduated in medicine in 1944. From 1951 to 1954, as a Fulbright Scholar in New York, he researched the role of stress in thyroid disease. After a further period of time in London, he returned in 1956 to the University of Adelaide, Department of Medicine. He was later appointed Professor of Medicine at the newly established Queen Elizabeth Hospital. In 1968, he was appointed Foundation Professor of Social and Preventive Medicine at Monash University. He became one of the Australian pioneers in 'new public health'. Later Dr Hetzel became the inaugural Chief of the CSIRO Division of Human Nutrition. In the 1960s, he led research in Papua New Guinea that identified the association between iodine deficiency and significant brain damage in unborn children. Through effectively lobbying the United Nations (UN), the global prevention of this immense problem has become his major life work, still continuing, and most of this has been achieved since 'retirement'. Dr Hetzel has also been Chancellor of the University of South Australia (1992–1998) and is at present the Lieutenant Governor of South Australia.

We were seated in the sitting room of Professor Hetzel's stately North Adelaide home, fresh flowers perfumed the air and framed watercolours and embroidery adorned the walls.

One can question 'retirement'. In a sense I retired from full-time work in 1986, from my position with the Commonwealth Scientific and Industrial Research Organisation (CSIRO), but I am now engaged quite fully in a variety of activities. I am seventy-six years old, and people tell me that I ought to be doing less, but I'm coping, I consider, fairly well with the activities and responsibilities that I have.

Of course I get tired, and I recognise my mental processes are not quite as good as they used to be. I have a short rest in the middle of the day. Three days a week I'm in my office, down the road at the Women's and Children's Hospital, and the two other days are flexible and based at home. Some of the time at home is taken up with formal work, and some with recreation, as well as domestic chores!

These days my main activity is as the chairman of an inter-national nutrition group that consults for the UN on iodine deficiency. Iodine deficiency has been an interest of mine for many years since the 1960s, but it was only when I retired from the CSIRO that I was really able to devote myself to this work. The group comprises 450 multi-disciplinary professionals from eighty countries with a majority from developing countries.

I'd been involved in research in the field, first of all in New Guinea, in the 1960s, when my team showed that iodine defi-ciency caused brain damage to the unborn child of the iodine deficient mother that can be prevented totally by correcting the deficiency before pregnancy. At that time, I was Professor of Medicine at the Queen Elizabeth Hospital and worked very closely with the Public Health Department in Papua New Guinea. We were fortunate to be able to do that study, which extended over nearly five years. That was the most important single piece of work with which I've been associated. There had been a lot of controversy about the problem before then.

When I started the new Division of Human Nutrition at CSIRO in Adelaide in 1976, we did further work that confirmed the effect of iodine deficiency on the brains of sheep and monkeys. The weight of the brain was less, due to a smaller number of cells, and the brain developed more slowly. So when I retired from the CSIRO, I decided I should try to do something to help countries with this problem, which was of a massive dimension. Iodine deficiency is now recognised by the World Health Organisation (WHO) as the most common preventable cause of brain damage in the world today.

We actually formed an international consultancy group, called the International Council for Control of Iodine Deficiency Disorders, in 1986 at Kathmandu, Nepal. I was the executive director for ten years, and I have been the chairman since 1995, which will continue until 2001, all being well, after which I will retire from that position. I've told my colleagues, and we've made arrangements for adapting to my absence, so to speak. I've been the treasurer since 1986. We've had the international auditor in recently, routinely reviewing our accounts, as I'm handling US$500,000 to US$600,000 a year, from various international agencies, including AusAid. I have to pay honoraria to people all over the world, and it all goes quite smoothly with only occasional hiccoughs.

I have a very good colleague who took over from me as the executive director. There is a small group of very distinguished scientific colleagues who are committed to this work. It's a fairly unusual thing, you see, for scientists to come out of the woodwork and commit themselves to making things happen in the developing world. So the work is becoming quite well known, as is the 'model' we have used where an expert, non-government group is recognised by the UN system to advise on this global program with the aim of eliminating iodine deficiency as a cause of brain damage by the year 2000.

We work very closely with WHO, and the United Nations International Children's Emergency Fund (UNICEF) in particular, but also with governments. I have a particularly close relationship with China, where I've been involved since 1981. In China there is an enormous problem with iodine deficiency, with forty per cent of its population at risk, as I discovered in 1981–1982 when I travelled all over that country. Since then, I've been continuously involved, with more than twelve trips to China.

Our group reviewed the program in 1989, and then I was asked by the Chinese Ministry of Health to chair an international agencies working group to coordinate their work in China. Subsequently, the World Bank made a very big grant to China for restructuring the salt industry – US$29 million. This led to a remarkable meeting in the Great Hall of the People in 1993, sponsored by the Premier of China, Li Peng. The government accepted this work as a top priority because of the importance of preventing brain damage to future generations.

Brain damage caused by iodine deficiency in the mother can be prevented, but it can't be corrected when it occurs at the foetal stage. So, in the most extreme form, there is brain damage with deaf-mutism and a spastic state of the legs. A most appalling handicap! It was first described in Europe in the Middle Ages, mostly in the mountains such as the European Alpine region. Some villages in Switzerland were severely affected, but also neighbouring villages in France, Germany and Italy. The term 'cretin' was used to describe sufferers.

Goitre, a swelling of the thyroid gland, is a common feature of iodine deficiency, and this took up all the scientific attention. Doctors had studied this great big gland in the neck for a hundred years, but the foetal brain damage from iodine deficiency in the mother was not recognised. My contribution really has been to demonstrate the effect on the foetal brain and that it can be prevented.

Various methods of prevention are used, but the most common by far is iodised salt. It was adopted in Australia after the second world war as a voluntary measure to prevent goitre. But the problem of iodine deficient foetal brain damage is so serious in the developing countries that many have made salt iodisation mandatory: all salt for human consumption has to be iodised. China, India, Brazil, and Indonesia have done that, as well as many others. As I have already said, my particular interest has been in China and also Indonesia, both of which I have visited many times since 1976.

It can be debated whether iodised salt should be mandatory in Australia. We do have other sources of iodised salt in a diversity of food, whilst most of these other countries have large populations living on subsistence agriculture. Australia, until after the war, had quite a lot of goitre, especially in areas like Tasmania, the Adelaide Hills, and throughout the Great Dividing Range.

Iodine deficiency has largely vanished in Australia, not because of iodised salt, but because of iodised milk. There has been iodine in our milk because iodofors were used in the dairy industry as a disinfectant. This has been true for probably thirty years, but iodofors are now being phased out because of cost. So, the iodine nutrition status in developed countries, where this disinfectant has been phased out, is suddenly becoming a matter of concern.

In Australia, iodine deficiency persisted longest in Tasmania. I have been involved in monitoring the situation for over thirty years. We can determine the status of iodine nutrition very conveniently by measuring the concentration of iodine in the urine. Usually this is in school children eight to ten years old. We've done some tests in Tasmania recently, and the tests indicate that the levels are getting quite low. We know how low they are when brain damage occurs, you see. So the tests are indicating some hazard, and my colleagues, assisted by me, have had to lobby the Minister of Health in Tasmania about this. With a change of government, you have to start again. It's the same in China!

You have to be involved both with the scientific and political process. In some ways it's a rather messy business. You have to accept a degree of frustration. Working in the UN is no picnic, I can assure you. It's not a 'drawing room exercise'. You've got to work with people who are not always that easy to get on with, but they're there, and there's no alternative. However, I do have a number of very good colleagues.

Being an Australian in the international arena has its advantages and disadvantages. It's not easy to be in Europe or America at short notice but, on the other hand, we are free of the imperialist baggage that the British and the Americans carry. They more or less push people around, unconsciously almost! We don't do that, and we are more acceptable in general as a result. In order to be able to work as I have, I think it's been a help to be Australian.

Also I've been able to do the things I've done because of the wonderful support I receive from Anne, who's my second wife. My first wife, Helen, whom I met as a student (we married in 1946), was also a wonderful support. As was common in a former generation, Helen took the main responsibility for family and our five children, while I pursued a very consuming life in medicine. Tragically, I lost Helen in 1980 from cancer. Fortunately I was able to marry again after three years, very happily. So, I've indeed been greatly blessed.

Anne has done quite a lot of travelling with me, in China and elsewhere, over the last fifteen years. Once a year we try to take a 'side-trip' for pleasure. We were in China in October last year, travelling with Chinese friends in eastern China, down to Shanghai from Beijing, where we observed the remarkable changes that have occurred since the 1980s. There was a consultation in Beijing with the Ministry of Health. All thirty-one provinces were represented, with one hundred and fifty people from all over China reporting on eliminating iodine deficiency. The progress with universal salt iodisation was remarkable – eighty per cent of the population now have access to iodised salt, compared to only forty per cent five years ago.

China has an authoritarian-style bureaucracy, which lends itself to public health. The order goes out from Beijing to all the provinces, and they comply. One exception is Tibet where, of course, there are difficulties. The other is the western province of Xinjiang, where there's a certain amount of unrest with a big Muslim population. They both have very severe iodine deficiency, but in due course it will come under control.

As it must be with these things, the timing was right. I was helped by the former head of UNICEF, a charismatic American named Jim Grant, whom I first met in New York during 1984. Jim died four years ago, greatly mourned. In 1984, the maternal iodine deficiency effect on babies was not perceived as the problem that it is. Jim saw the problem, and UNICEF have been very supportive of the program. UNICEF has over one hundred and sixty offices in countries throughout the world, so this makes a big difference. They took special responsibility for the iodisation of salt and getting satisfactory salt iodising machines into all these countries. This involves engineering challenges, and logistical problems, which have been overcome to a remarkable extent.

Jim Grant was also the key architect of the World Summit for Children at the UN in 1990 when seventy-one heads of state met and eighty-eight other governments signed a declaration for a new order of health and education for children. This declaration included the elimination of the iodine deficiency problem by the year 2000. This has provided important political support for national programs.

My motivation for this work is basically a form of humanitarianism that I acquired originally as a medical student, when I became a committed Christian. This has continued to influence my life. I don't go to church every Sunday, but I go regularly every four weeks or so, when we attend Pilgrim Church in the city. I was connected with the Presbyterian Church originally. Earlier I was at King's College, which started as a non-conformist Congregational Baptist school. The Student Christian Movement (SCM) was an important influence upon me at university.

You see, when I was at Adelaide University during the war, in the 1940s, there was only a small student community (medical studies was a reserved occupation). That experience of mixing with other students, and the involvement with SCM, provided me with a liberal education that has made quite a difference over the years. It gave me more of a social conscience too. Some of my medical and scientific colleagues are not so 'broad'.

The three days at the office are principally to deal with the iodine deficiency program. In addition, I have been Chancellor of the University of South Australia and since completing my term in 1998, I have remained associated with the university in relation to the Bob Hawke Prime Ministerial Centre, which became operational at the beginning of 1998. This Centre includes first of all a library for the life and times of Bob Hawke, modelled on the Presidential Libraries in the US. Bob Hawke is very cooperative and committed to the project, and I keep in touch with him because I'm chairman of the fundraising committee. We have a substantial target of twenty million dollars for a building program to not only provide for the library, but also for a research institute.

A number of the university's research groups have come in under the umbrella of the Hawke Centre. They research areas such as social justice, gender issues, Aboriginal issues, and work place issues. In addition, there is a community education project about major national issues. I see the Centre as making a major contribution to a better awareness of Australia's identity among the younger generation.

My other responsibility is as Lieutenant Governor of South Australia. I have had the privilege of working closely with Dame Roma Mitchell while she was Governor, and since then with Sir Eric Neal. In this role, I deputise when the Governor is not in Adelaide, particularly as chairman of the Executive Council. The Executive Council meets every week to approve new legislation, and also proclamations and appointments. It meets rain or shine, fifty weeks of the year. So, if the Governor is interstate or overseas, I 'act' in the role. Also I attend some functions when the Governor is here as, of course, he's very busy indeed, and he can't do everything that is requested.

The Queen appoints Governors and Lieutenant Governors individually for the states of Australia. This is an issue, obviously, in relation to the future and the possibility of Australia becoming a republic, and so on. In Australia, we have a tradition of the states being independent principalities, which differs from Canada.

In the early 1970s, South Australia changed the long-standing tradition of the chief justice being the Lieutenant Governor. When Don Dunstan appointed Dr John Bray as chief justice, he didn't want to be Lieutenant Governor as well. He pointed out that it confused executive and judicial functions. Obviously, an alternative had to be found, and so Sir Walter Crocker, a distinguished retired diplomat, now well over ninety, was appointed. After ten years, he was followed by the late Sir Condor Laucke, from whom I took over in 1992.

These three positions keep me pretty well fully occupied. Well, I do have a bit of time for recreation, but not as much as I would like. I like reading history and biography. Although I've got a substantial number of books, and many are biographies and history, I never seem to get enough time to read. My wife is a voracious reader and is able to read a lot more than I can in the general arena, while I have to battle on with the various things I really have to read in connection with the work that I do. Slowly that is changing.

I'm conscious of the ageing process in that I recognise how I forget things, especially recent events. I need to keep little notes, and also a diary for appointments. This is absolutely essential, but I'm more forgetful now than I was three years ago, I have to admit. Therefore, I have to take more precautions so I don't overlook anything. It's not a problem with the work I do, as far as I am aware, as I can cope by taking enough care. I seem to remember the iodine issues fairly well. I have two part-time secretaries, about four days a week altogether. They're wonderful.

You're also more aware of limitations, the need to manage time, and to prepare adequately for what comes along. The appointments, ceremonies and so on, all have to be fitted in, so my diary is a very important 'right hand' to planning. I plan reasonably well, better than I would have managed twenty years ago. One has to have enough energy when the time comes for something. In special circumstances of course, you get very involved and can keep going, but when I want to work on a paper, I like to do it in the morning, fresh, before too many things have distracted me.

As one ages, it is possible to take a somewhat more detached view of things, you know. There are limits to what can be achieved, and one accepts the limitations of one's situation. I think that you can take a more balanced view of situations and not demand the impossible of yourself or others. It makes no sense to be sighing after the impossible.

Music is a great joy for me. I tried to keep playing the piano, but gave it up quite a long time ago as a student. You could say that I was enthusiastic, rather than skilled. I was very keen about it, and I'm very fond of piano music. That is an important resource in my life, especially the classics: Schubert, Bach, Beethoven and Mozart. I'm not a passionate consumer of modern music, I must admit, but some of it is attractive.

My wife is an artist. Anne paints but she's particularly known for embroidery. She has been SA President of the Embroiderer's Guild and is now involved in setting up a national textile museum at Urrbrae, a campus of the University of Adelaide. Anne's done a lot of work in relation to our travels, especially China, India, and Russia. Here on the walls there are embroidered Russian motifs and Buddhist motifs that demonstrate her great talent.

We have a large family between us, and our life is fairly family-oriented. There are eleven children, each with families; five of the eleven are here in Adelaide, four interstate, with two overseas. We do travel interstate to visit, overseas also, and we see quite a bit of the local family. A fair bit of time is spent on interstate and international phone calls. We like it that way as we are then in regular touch.

One does get involved with the ups and downs of family life. We have quite a big house on the coast at Carrickalinga, on a hill overlooking the bay, with a wonderful view. That's the family gathering place for holidays. Quite a few gather for Christmas. We had a special celebration for my seventy-fifth birthday when we hired six houses for the visitors, which all worked out very happily. The gathering included forty-two 'souls' over a great variety of ages! We have thirty-four grand-children between us.

When we first purchased the house at Carrickalinga, over twenty years ago, I would go fishing, but not these days. We walk on the beach and also visit friends down there, and we have entertained many overseas and interstate visitors there. There are quite a lot of books and I have a stereo.

We have a subscription to Musica Viva, chamber music, with eight concerts in Adelaide a year, although we can't always attend. Occasionally, we go to the theatre and other concerts as well. However, both of us are a bit deaf, so we find that it's not so easy to hear plays anymore.

I don't exercise in any systematic way. I mean, we walk, but that's about all. There was a time when I used to ride a stationary bicycle. It's still upstairs, but I don't do it these days, I'm afraid. I would say that I certainly don't take enough exercise, but I am encouraged by the recent gentler recommendation of walking for thirty minutes a day, which I almost meet.

I've been very fortunate in that I have not really stopped working. Occasionally I get a bit frustrated – no time and too busy and whatnot – but you can't have everything! Some of my colleagues, my contemporaries in medicine, just don't have much to do at all, and there are moments when that seems attractive, when you're too busy.

The iodine work, I have to admit, was 'an extra' when I took it on originally, in 1964. I was too busy anyway, but I took it on mainly because of a humanitarian commitment. I thought I really *should* do it even though it seemed to be too much, and to some extent it was. My wife assisted in paying that price, as I was away, to and fro, to New Guinea. I was also on the University Council for seven years from 1965. I was up and down to New Guinea four times a year for the Council Meetings, but could keep an eye on the research!

There were some other things I took on at that time too, including an organisation called Australia Frontier that was established by the Australian Council of Churches in 1962. Australia Frontier was concerned with the issues of rapid urban development and helped to establish community life in new housing areas. Here in South Australia, Elizabeth was the classical example. This was a very considerable commitment also over the years 1963–1972, but it did open my eyes to the broader dimension of health and illness in social and community terms. This was a factor leading to my appointment, in 1968, at Monash University as Foundation Professor of Social and Preventive Medicine.

From Monash, I gave the ABC Boyer Lectures in 1971 on 'Life and Health in Australia'. It was a big surprise to be asked to do those lectures, but I'd had a fair amount of media exposure before that, talking about health in social, psychological and spiritual terms. This was concerning the 'new' public health, as opposed to drains and the like, which was the nineteenth-century, physical environment type of public health. I was concerned with lifestyle and the social environment. The lectures led to a book, a Penguin publication, *Health in*

Australian Society, which sold nearly forty thousand copies and became a standard text for students in the health and social sciences.

A lot of medicine is predicated on the concept of the body as a machine. That aspect is very important, but it's not the whole story. I developed an approach to health from a broad psycho-social perspective. For me, this was based on a spiritual concept of man made in the image of God, and not just a machine, and it went on from there. I'd been long interested in theology, and had done a formal course in New York with the famous theologian Paul Tillich when I was there from 1951 to 1954. At that point, my work was on stress problems. In New York I met the English poet, WH Auden, who was also interested in the connections between theology, medicine and psychiatry.

I continue to have an active interest in this area. You would find quite a lot of theology books on my shelves, mixed up with histories of philosophy and science. What I first learnt about as a student (and it's been with me all my life) is a type of thinking called 'process thought' that is very anti the rationalist perspective, which is so dominant today. So, for instance, when I was at the Queen Elizabeth Hospital, I was committed to establishing a multi-disciplinary approach to care. As part of that, I was involved in representations to the Methodist Church, which led to a full-time chaplaincy service there in 1960.

My father was a distinguished physician and Dean of the Medical School at Adelaide University when it expanded in the 1950s. He was certainly quite an influence, a considerable influence. He was very passionate about medical research, and encouraged me in this direction. He was a country boy, descended from Silesian migrants who developed the Barossa Valley. My grandfather had a cheese factory near Tanunda.

My father was awarded scholarships and, as a medical student, graduated top of his year in 1920. He worked until he was eighty, and died at the age of eighty-one.

The most important decision I made, in retrospect, was to move from clinical medicine to public health, which is what I did when I went to Monash University in Melbourne. I let the clinical medicine arena go, not without regret. On the other hand, the opportunities I've had in public health have been really much more meaningful and bigger challenges, but consuming. Quite consuming!

When one is older, it is important to have meaning for your life, and the opportunity of doing meaningful things. I think that people who have very consuming hobbies are very fortunate, especially as an alternative for fairly humdrum activities. I suppose I haven't had a lot of time to spare for a consuming hobby, rightly or wrongly, and I recognise that I have put most of myself into my work. Other people don't put as much in, and they've got more left over for other things, and I see the advantages of that. But medicine is a very consuming game and I don't regret it because I feel I've been fortunate to have such rich opportunities.

So, my advice to other men about ageing is that life still needs to be meaningful. But meaning is a highly individual thing. In other words, meaning can be very diverse and arise from hobbies, or studying with the University of the Third Age, or simply from the joys and up and downs of family life.

I suppose I'm interested in ideas. Study is something I find naturally congenial, but whether I'll get around to doing a formal course in philosophy or history, I don't quite know. I'd be happy to do a bit of work in theology, a little bit of work in history, with a philosophical or theological tinge to it, like the Reformation. I read a book over Christmas: Bryan Magee's

Confessions of a Philosopher, which I enjoyed. I keep several books going at once, but often do not finish them!

My view is that, first of all, the social environment is very important at all ages, and that improving the social environment is, to a degree, a government responsibility. It is also an individual responsibility, but I think the individual has limitations. It has to be seen as a community responsibility, but including government. So we need appropriate facilities for older people.

Secondly, as I've said in lectures, ageing people have a lot to contribute to society and it's in the interests of the community at large to make sure that older people have a chance to make their contribution. Of course, the old stereotypes have to be discarded first.

In an address to the 7th National Meals on Wheels Conference, held in 1997, I emphasised that older people are givers and not takers, healthier than ever before, no longer needing nursing home beds in the numbers required in the past, and enjoying a richer quality of life than ever before. I also said that older people are needed to provide a steadying influence in a time of rapid change by asserting spiritual values and meaning for life at both personal and social levels.

There has been a dramatic increase in life expectancy since 1950, due mainly to the fall in mortality from coronary heart disease. Recently I heard that this is increasing by a year every three years. It's really an unprecedented phenomenon. In another of my books, *The LS Factor* (about the lifestyle factor and health), there is a diagram that shows very clearly the mortality rate improvement from the beginning of the century. It started with the improvement in infant mortality, and then there was a plateau during the 1950s and the 1960s, after which it again started to improve.

We did a lot of work at the CSIRO on the relation of diet to health pertaining to heart disease and the importance of the switch from butter to margarine in Australia since the 1960s. We showed this epidemiologically at the population level, but then we followed it with experimental work in animal models indicating how a diet high in saturated fat was associated with the heart being more likely to develop an arrhythmia and stop. A big feature of this fall in mortality has been the fall in sudden death in Australia, as in the United States, and elsewhere.

Some people are saying that life expectancy could go to a hundred or a hundred and twenty years. Okay, we know more about cardiovascular disease, and it's amazing that the knowledge we have is sufficient to be so beneficial in its effects, but in the case of the brain, we have a long way to go. Dementia is now a major unsolved problem.

Another lifestyle factor for men is whether they live alone or not. Having a very compatible partner (in our case it's marriage) and very good comradeship and friendship, makes an *enormous* difference. The fact is that men who are alone die sooner and have more health problems. That's the way it is, as social beings, humans generally need supportive relationships for health and wellbeing. So I've been blessed in every way by having had meaningful work and two very happy marriages.

When I do have more time, there might be a bit of travelling for pleasure, but I have travelled more than a million miles since 1981 in the cause of freedom from iodine deficiency. You become aware of the inconvenience of travelling as the years go by, especially the business of flying. Also, there are so many people everywhere at major tourist resorts. One of our grandchildren had two months in northern Italy recently. When she visited Venice, the place was *stuffed* with tourists, and we're talking about winter – January! Well, I'm happier to read a book about Venice with some nice pictures, in comfort, in the armchair.

We might spend more time down at the beach house. It's very peaceful down there – very peaceful indeed. I will be quite happy to spend much more time down there, reading and enjoying the sea and the sky always changing.

It has been good, however, to be able to just continue meaningful work. I've been able, to a degree, to bypass the problem of ageing. I mean, my life's been able to continue. If I hadn't had this major interest over these later years, I admit that I could have found life very difficult. I've always worked hard you see, and to just stop like that, would have been quite a problem. That hasn't happened to me so far, although to some extent it will happen in a couple of years' time. But, of course, I'm much older than I was at the age of sixty-three when I retired from the CSIRO. That's thirteen years ago and I've had this wonderful time since. It's really, in some ways, been the most satisfying part of my life.

THE OLD MAN AND THE FISH

Nick Angelakis

A well-known and busy spot in the Adelaide Central Market is the Angelakis Brothers shop, which sells fresh seafood, poultry and game. This business, founded some years ago by George and Nikitas Angelakis, immigrants to Australia from Symi in the Greek Isles in 1936, has expanded successfully to other sites. Nick is the surviving brother, and although the business is now managed by the next generation, he remains involved in the day-to-day activity of getting seafood to the customer. Considered by the local Greek Community to be an example of ageing well, Nick's life, despite considerable health challenges, continues to be centred on his family and his work with fish.

Nick arrived from the fish factory across the road, removed his rubber boots and showed us into his son's office at the Angelakis Brothers headquarters for this interview.

I'm seventy-seven going on seventy-eight, but I can't stop! I just feel like working, you know. It keeps you occupied, and well, you feel a lot better. I feel better if I'm busy, really I do. I don't think I'll ever stop, not as far as I'm concerned at present. I used to work full-time, but I gave it up when I had an operation about three years ago. For about the last two or three years I have only worked up to about midday, from Monday to Friday, and I have the weekend off as far as work is concerned.

It's early, about five in the morning, when I get ready. Then I come down to the factory and go with my son Tom to the wholesale market where we buy all the fish that we want. That's what I do. We've got friends there, and we joke a bit and all that, and laugh. That makes you feel good. And then we come over to the factory and sometimes I start filleting, if they are short-handed. I decide what we have got to fillet and what we have to sell whole. From previous experience I can see what has to be done.

Starting at about the age of fifteen, I fished for twenty-five years on the West Coast of South Australia, at Thevenard. Our boat, mind you, was a thirty-five foot boat, so we were not really big fishermen. We used to fish with a smaller boat, camping on the bigger boat. We'd stay out for about three or four days, or maybe five, until there were enough fish caught, whiting mainly, then go in and sell them. We used to keep the fish alive in the water of the boat, so the fish, when we used to bring them in, were jumping out of the boxes! The wholesalers there used to take the whole lot – no trouble selling them. Then we formed a cooperative. My brother was involved mostly, but all the family was involved, and since then, we fishermen have never looked back.

My brother George happened to get a bit sick and he

came down to Adelaide and got the shop in the Market – the one that we've got at present. So I had to come down myself in 1960. Since then we've had the shop in the Market and this wholesale business. The boys took over about four or five years ago, and they have extended the business quite a lot. It now employs ninety-five people.

With a lot of other businesses I have noticed that having younger men take over is alright, if they're knowledgeable. It's good if they get the old people's opinion, because they still have got a lot to learn. They think they know, but they don't know all of it yet.

We came out here from the Dhodhekanisos Islands. It's a group of twelve islands, and Symi is the one we come from. It's close to Rhodes Island. After the first world war, the islands came under Italian control, and then when the last war finished, they were given back to Greece. Most of the islands are along Asia Minor.

My father made two trips to Australia. The first time he went to Port Augusta and worked in the salt works there for six years, and came home to Symi in 1930. I was born when he was away. I didn't really know my father until he came back. He stopped for about six months and then left for Australia again, but he couldn't go back to the old job at the salt works, so he went fishing. Then he sent for us. There was my mum, Anna, my brother George, and my sister Evagelina.

I left school and was thirteen when I came out to Australia. After attending the local school in Ceduna for about a year and a half, I left and started fishing. There was no other work I'd rather do, so I had to go fishing. On Symi, some of us boys used to do a little bit of fishing. In fact, one year we got twenty-five big fish. The older ones reckoned even the professional fishermen couldn't catch fish like that!

When we were fishing out from Thevenard, we used to have fish every night on the boat. I like eating fish and I still do. Garfish is a nice fish. The other fish are mainly the same, but garfish has got a different taste altogether. Grilled garfish gets a bit dry, so fried is best, with a bit of flour on it. Vegetable oil is very good. Olive oil is a little heavy, but vegetable oil is a bit lighter. With the little ones, it's good to just cut the head off, gut them, and fry them whole. When you eat them, you just split them open, get all the meat out, and you've left all the bone behind.

At home, I have a garden with quite a lot of roses to look after, and that's what I do in the afternoon. If I have nothing to do, even on Sundays, I usually work out in the garden. Well, there's nothing else for me to do! Don't go anywhere, hardly ever go anywhere.

I've got quite a few roses, and I've had them since I bought the house up in the hills in 1970. We used to live down on the Port Road, in one of a pair of maisonettes. George was living in one and me in the other, but the family was growing, so I had to get a house. I had the rose bushes given to me, so they're just there, that's it. They are all different colours. There's a nice yellow rose, and there's a red – not very red, not the dark red, but it's got a beautiful perfume, that one. Another is an orangey colour, and that has a lovely perfume. Oh, a very nice perfume!

Living up in the hills though, once that gully wind blows, it spoils your roses, making them shrivel up, especially in the hot weather. With roses, you've got to look after them, and you've got to water them well on hot days, but I water them every day and still the heat affects them. If you're in a sheltered place, then it's good. So, water them every day and you've got good roses, but not if you get the gully wind and hot weather!

The only reading that I do is the paper. When I watch the telly, it is mainly sports, like football and tennis. The football team that I follow nowadays is the Crows, of course! It used to be Port Adelaide, as we came from the West Coast, which was a district where Port Adelaide picked players. Now I watch the Crows on the TV. I don't follow soccer very much, but football every time. Every time.

Since I came down to Adelaide from Thevenard, I've fished a bit, as we had a little motor boat from which we used to go fishing if there was good weather on the weekend. We used to go along the coast a bit, sometimes to catch squid, mostly squid, and some red mullet. Just a few whiting, as there are not many whiting here, but there are lots up the West Coast. I haven't been fishing for a long, long time. The boys were not so interested and the boat was too heavy for me to handle, so we sold it.

My health is not too bad now. I don't mind telling you that I had a growth removed on the bowel. That was nearly four years ago. And then one day I went for dinner some-where, and when I had to go up the steps I started to get a bit of pain. I thought, 'Well, it's indigestion,' but it kept on going all the time. I told the boys: 'Look, I've got some pain. I don't know what it is, but I get indigestion so I think it will be alright.' The boys kept on saying, 'No, we have to go and see the doctor,' and I went to the doctor about nine o'clock that night.

We went to St Andrew's, and when I told them the trouble I had, straight away they had me checked. They sent a specialist. It happened to be my brother's specialist too, because he had a by-pass – a coronary by-pass operation. The specialist said, 'I think you had a mild heart attack,' and so they kept me for seven days at St Andrew's. I went for an angiogram, and he said, 'You've got two arteries half closed and one altogether blocked.' So he said that I should have the by-pass operation.

It was alright, but the funny part was that on the same day there were another two having the same operation – a lady and a man. The man had a very bad heart and he didn't get through it. I felt sorry for the poor fellow because the three of us were together when the doctor talked to us about what they were going to do and all that. The woman was first, and she was alright. Then I was second and the other fellow was third. He kept fighting for a couple of days, and that was it. He passed away.

I'm okay now. I walk every day for about an hour up the Morialta Reserve. On the weekend, the walking is first thing in the morning. On an ordinary day, I walk in the afternoon after I finish with the fish. I started walking after my heart operation, but I wish I had started before that. You know, I used to see people walking and think, 'Oh, those silly people walking first thing in the morning, losing all their sleep!' It's a different story when you've got to do it yourself!

Also, I'm very careful about what I eat. I was very careful before the operation too, as I had an upset tummy from spicy foods, which I now don't like in my diet. I eat very light food, and I don't touch coffee except that I might have a very light Nescafé. Usually I have a Milo – that's all. Well, lately I've been having a little red wine. They say it's good for you, so sometimes I have that, but not always.

My wife, Tsambica, is not from the same island as me, but the one next-door, Rhodes Island. Her father brought her here, and her mother too. She's got three brothers, but they were here in Australia before her. I met my wife over in Thevenard, and we've been married since 27 August 1952.

We've got two boys, Michael and Tom, and two girls, Anna and Desi. First were the boys, and the two girls afterwards. There are eight grandchildren, four of each: four boys and four girls. Usually, every weekend, they come up to visit. One, at least, comes every Sunday. I look forward to that. They have tea or dinner, whatever, and then they go home. Well, the children make a mess of the house, but you don't mind that. Being a grandfather keeps you happy. I've got a young daughter who's married to a chappie in Sydney, and we go there every year for about four weeks.

I tell you, in the Greek Community, with our children, when they are very young they are spoilt a lot by the parents, but when the children get older, they respect their parents. You would find that at least ninety per cent of them respect their parents. They look after them too. When the Australian kids are young, you couldn't wish for better kids, but when they get to a certain age, they sort of get out of the family. It is the opposite with us. Even when they get married, they bring their children and have dinner.

The wider family, the nieces and nephews, they are the same. We go to visit and they come to visit us. We used to have Christmas all together, but the families are grown up now. Every family has got grandchildren, and it's a bit hard. Sometimes we do it, though. Mind you, we celebrate 'Name Day'. They all come, or we go to theirs, but we don't celebrate birthdays very much, except for the young generation. The kids do, but the older people, no. We celebrate our Name Day, like St Nikitas Day for me, or St Jude, or St Michael.

I only go to the church if I have to go! I go if it is Easter time, or if there is a Christening or a wedding that we are invited to, but that's about all. We have a very good old folk's home run by the Greek Orthodox Community, and it has been judged by the Federal government as one of the best in South Australia. You know, that's a very good thing they've done, very good, because it's not only for the Greek old people, there's even Australians.

Just as well my father brought us all out to Australia when he did. During the war, God knows what would have happened to us; no help from anybody. I don't know how I would have got on. It would have been very bad, but we were lucky, and in May 1936, we came to Australia.

Being a migrant in the beginning was not the same as it is now. Now, the Australians and all the migrants, they all get together, but not before. It's different now. You feel more at home than you used to in those days. Mind you, it's since the war that things have started to go the other way around. In the early days it was a bit hard.

In 1983 I went back to Symi. That was after forty-seven years. They are beautiful islands, especially our little island. Symi isn't colourful, but it's very quiet, and it's a nice place to go for a holiday. If you want a quiet place, that's it. Rhodes Island is a bit crowded with a lot of tourism. Thousands and thousands of people! I went back again in 1987, when we went right around the world with my niece and her family.

It was interesting to go back, but I don't mind telling you, you've got relatives there and yet, after a long time to go and see them, you don't feel like you are at home. You go with all the pleasure to see them, and when you see them, you lose interest. They forget about you, maybe because of the many years, but you don't forget them just because you are in a different country. You go to your own country and see all those people, even school mates, and you say, 'Don't you remember me?' Mind you, everybody who leaves from here comes back with the same impression.

It was hard work that made us successful. Even the boys, they are working very hard. Hard work and selling good fish, because that's also a main reason too – quality. In the early 1980s the families talked about raising money for charity, and in 1983 we held our first 'Seafood Affair' in conjunction with Yalumba Winery, TAA, Channel 10, and others. All of the family helped by preparing platters, making sweets, and cooking. People from other organisations also helped. Over the years there have been some changes – Channel 9 is now a sponsor. We have helped raise nearly $250,000. Everyone enjoys the day and tickets are sold almost a year ahead.

I used to get up at five o'clock in the morning and work through a full day. On Tuesdays I used to get up that early, then work until five o'clock down the shop. On Fridays, before the boys took over the shop, when there was my brother, brother-in-law and me, we used to get up at three in the morning and work until six o'clock at night. When Friday late-night shopping started, we used to work up to nine o'clock! It was long hours – very, very long hours.

I never think about getting older. The longer you do that, the better it is, and that's why I never think I'm old. You always think you are the same, or that's what I do anyway. You always think that you are young, but that's not the case, especially when you get some health troubles. That makes you worry a little bit, but if you get all worried, then you go back again.

You can't do any heavy work, but you should do a little bit of work – not too much. Well, you can have a bit of time to yourself after work. As far as I'm concerned, I think you should work a bit. It keeps you occupied and keeps your mind there.

A SIMPLER PALETTE

Ian George

The Most Reverend Dr Ian George has been the Anglican Archbishop of Adelaide since 1991. Educated at St Peter's College and the University of Adelaide, he practiced law before altering course to attend the General Theological Seminary in New York, to then be ordained in New York as Deacon and Priest in the Cathedral of St John the Divine in 1964. Since his return to Australia in 1965, he has had numerous prestigious and pivotal roles within the Anglican Church in South Australia, Western Australia, Queensland, and the Australian Capital Territory. For many years he has been involved in four main areas: the arts, government and community bodies, education and media, and welfare agencies. This involvement occurs at local, national, and international levels, through work associated with membership and leadership of government and church committees. His belief in being involved in the community is evident from his position as Co-patron of the Port Power Football Club. Archbishop George was made a member of the Order of Australia in 1989.

We visited the Anglican Archbishop's residence to speak to him and entered a room decorated with art and bookcases, to sit around a ten-seat table on leather-bound chairs.

As you age, it is quite fascinating to watch what happens to your skin. I'm just beginning to get this sort of 'gathering'. My weight doesn't change, but I recognise that my body shape is, so my belt's not as tight as it used to be. It's sort of slipping down.

There's a little chalet up in the Victorian Alps that we love to go to, and when we were on holidays recently, for the first time I actually sat in front of the mirror and sketched myself. That was a *very* interesting experience. One of my great loves, regarding art, is the series of Rembrant self-portraits. There are four of them in one little room in a museum in Vienna, and I think they take him from about thirty to his early sixties. I've spent a lot of time just sitting and looking at those portraits. There before you is the whole process of ageing and wisdom.

It's also very interesting when you look at the lives of the great artists and you see how their work becomes simpler as they get to the end of their lives. Their palette becomes more limited. With some great painters, Cèzanne is one, Moraudi is another, their palette actually becomes confined to fewer colours because they can do more, and they are challenging themselves to do more, with less. Now that seems to me to be a very interesting metaphor – 'doing more with less'.

The older and wiser we become, the more we become detached from material things. Don't ask my wife for any comment on that, because she says, 'We've got so much junk that we're going to have to move when we retire!' I've already started throwing things out, so we're on the path. But I think we become more concerned with people as people, rather than people as part of issues or projects or programming. Jung said, 'The first half of life is about self, and the second half of life is the opening to others.'

Most people become much more compassionate. It's very

interesting to see the average age of people who are generous contributors to the Christmas Bowl Appeal. The statistics suggest that the older age groups in the population are the most generous givers. I also know people who have become incredibly enriched in their views as they have aged. I think that these things are very Christ-like.

If the crucifixion had occurred later, it is interesting to contemplate Jesus as an old man. He died when he was about thirty-three, but what did he look like? It's also interesting that there's not one remaining picture of Jesus. We have paintings of a whole lot of Greco-Roman figures of that period, but there's no picture of Jesus. So if you're black, you can imagine him black. If you're pink, you can imagine him pink. However, he could have been one of two DNA strains of the Jewish race. The majority are dark-haired, swarthy-skinned, brown-eyed, or he could have been red-haired with blue eyes. The average height of a male, in that area then, was about 172 centimetres.

The average life expectancy of the people at the time would have been mid-forties. Jesus would obviously have been very fit because of the walking that he did, so he probably would have reached the life expectancy, maybe a bit more. So, if he had grown older, he would have been wiry and tough. But how different would he be than the way he is presented in the Gospels? I wouldn't have thought very different. I mean he had a marvellous capacity for gentleness and relating directly to the needs of the person concerned, but he also had a fiery, prophetic voice when he felt it was required.

Some wisdom comes with age, but we're always what we are and there's a sense in which the leopard can't change its spots. The strengths and weaknesses that we have, and they're usually the other sides of the same coin, tend to be accentuated with age, rather than changed with age. There's a sense in which we confirm our strengths, but we also confirm our weaknesses. And so, I think there's a certain wisdom that comes with age where we learn to make the best use of our strengths and ameliorate our weaknesses.

But the other thing I think happens as we get older is that we become more aware of ourselves. And so we become more honest about our agendas, and we can actually put them aside at times. Marriages work better, because there's no point in fighting that battle over again. If you really still have that agenda, you ask yourself if it is really important enough for a battle. I think the same thing applies to working relationships. The little things that might have been very irritating about people, you can work around. Alternatively, tolerance can be a weakness. It can be a refusal to grapple with an issue.

That's one of the things about ageing isn't it? You get to know yourself better. You know what you can do and what you can't do, and you develop a bit of an instinct for whether that's the right way to go or not, which is valuable, I think.

I'm a kind of creative thinker, an ideas person. Although I was trained as a lawyer and I can do the detailed stuff when I have to, these days I try to leave that to other people, and I try to look at the broad picture. I'm very much involved in international things. I chaired the International Affairs Commission of the Anglican Church in Australia for many years. I chair the Anglican Communion International Refugee and Migrant Network, and the Christian World Service Commission of the National Council of Churches, which runs the Christmas Bowl Appeal.

That appeal raises two to three million dollars a year, and with government subsidies, there is something like four or five million to dispose of overseas in maybe sixty-five countries.

That's a great joy for me, and I do a little bit of travelling for them that helps me to keep my feet on the ground, and to have a clear vision of what's happening. Last year, my wife and I had two fascinating weeks in refugee camps for Burmese people in Thailand. The Australian Government, through us, puts a lot of money into those camps, and they're amazingly well run, but that's just an example.

So I try and keep the broad perspective as much as I can, and I'm very interested in the history of ideas. I try to find time to read widely, because I know that my strength is to get a group of people together, and to facilitate and turn the group to brainstorming creative ideas for action. If I have to get buried working through balance sheets and a whole lot of detailed stuff, my mind just gets very tired, and I get fogged up. So that's the sort of thing you learn as you get older, and to which you adjust.

Generally speaking, I work from about 7.30 am until about 11.30 pm, but I'm getting older, nearly sixty-five, so I find it very beneficial to have a siesta for an hour after lunch these days. This enables me to keep up the pace; otherwise I couldn't do it. I was getting very weary in the middle of the afternoon and it was a low, non-productive period. Probably I was making some bad decisions at that time, and not focusing effectively, in interviews for example. A couple of times, to my shock and horror, I found myself drifting off to sleep while people were talking, which is a terribly embarrassing thing to do. And so I thought, 'This is not good enough!'

Organisation is absolutely crucial. I have always insisted on running my own diary because if you give your diary to some-body, and you let them fill in all the appointments, you just become a slave or a victim, and it's quite pointless. You've got to retain some degree of oversight and control over the way you use your time. My wonderful and invaluable secretary, who is my right arm and more like a 'personal assistant', does a tremendous amount for me, and is very tolerant of me, because I'm not always efficient.

I try to take one day off a week, which is Thursday. Other things sometimes encroach upon that day, but for one of the Thursdays each month, I try to paint with a group of friends. It's good fun. I've been an art critic for forty-five years, and I'm pleased to do something to try to develop my formal, technical skills, at this stage. I'd like to go on painting in retirement and make it a bit of a specialty.

My retirement age is set for seventy, so I retire in August 2004. Recently, for the first time, my wife and I met with our accountant and financial adviser to start planning for our retirement. We have started looking at potential retirement homes in the hills. We have a particular target, as we need to get a house this year. To our great joy, our daughter and her husband are coming to Adelaide to live for three years, and they can live in that house. They have one little daughter who is the 'apple of our eye', and our daughter is pregnant again, so they'll come with two kids, and we'll have them for three years.

I'm an only child and my parents are both dead. My wife's parents are both dead, and she has only one brother in the US. So our daughter and our granddaughter are absolutely central to our existence. I have to say that she's a great deal more central to my existence now than she was years ago. You know, I was one of those clergy who probably sacrificed their families, to a certain extent, for the sake of the ministry. There were times when my wife said, 'You're more willing to go out and help somebody in need who calls, than to recognise the needs that are right here!' That's a familiar story with clergy, of course.

I was brought up in Adelaide. My parents were sort of Christmas and Easter Anglicans, but I went to an Anglican school, and then I did what many did in those days, and I went on to the university and did law. Then I went into legal practice.

A bit earlier, when I was eighteen and in my first year of university, I had my first real intimation of a calling to this particular ministry. I went to see my old school chaplain, and he said, 'Oh, come back and see me in three months time,' which was very wise, because the calling disappeared. It took another eight, nine years to come out again. By that time I was well into legal practice, but you know, that's the way it went.

I had the enormous good fortune to be sent to New York to do my theological study. They offered me a scholarship for my tuition fees, which meant I could afford to go a year earlier. It was just so wonderful, and it all seemed so right. It was the most amazing opportunity as it was intellectually a lot more rigorous than anything in Australia. I lived right in the centre of Manhattan for three years and worked part-time in a slum parish, which really woke up a young, pampered Adelaide brat. That experience opened my eyes to what life's all about.

One of my motivations in becoming a candidate for ordination was that I saw Christianity as the one force that was likely to change the world and bring it together, and I wanted to be part of changing the world. Well, as you get older, you realise you're not going to change the world. You might change some of it, if you're very remarkable like Basil Hetzel with his work on iodine deficiency. He has transformed the lives of hundreds of thousands of people.

People asked: 'Why are you leaving the legal profession? You've got a lucrative future here.' I'd say, 'Well, I'm really looking for somebody for whom I can work happily for twenty-four hours a day, seven days a week.' That's exactly what I used to say, and that was it.

I think the church has an absolutely crucial function in all areas of social justice, but being the International Year of Older Persons, I think we've got to be particularly up front this year. Of course, together the churches do more about care of the aged than anyone else in the community, but we're all finding it extraordinarily difficult to cope with the changes in government policy and the financial demands.

The way in which the government is forcing us all to develop tendering processes for all these welfare contracts is not only diverting our energies into really short term activities, but engendering a mode of competition between the church agencies that is very, very unhealthy. The state minister is very aware of that, and doesn't want to see any more of this tendering, but what do you put in its place? The government's got limited resources, and we've got limited resources.

The Anglican Church has just built a state-of-the-art aged care facility, Dutton Court, at Elizabeth. Now, we could only do that because one of the Duttons left us a million and a quarter dollars. We will never be able to do that again unless people leave us large sums of money, because the big government grants have gone, and we're scrambling for every cent of ongoing recurrent grant.

I'm one of the team of Family Ambassadors for the state government, and we had a meeting recently because we're gearing up for a new phase, and the aged are part of this. They were asking me if I was going to be the Ambassador for the Aged, or whether we'd bring in somebody aged! I said, 'I'm quite happy to be the Ambassador for the Aged!'

Probably one of the big challenges facing all the mainstream churches in Australia today is the way in which the average age of the church-going community is increasing every year. Personally, I think we really ought to be focusing upon people when they start getting married and having kids. That's when they start developing some concern for the values of the family circle and all that stuff. But I don't have a sense of desperation about the future of the church. If God wants us to go on, we'll go on, and He'll find the ways.

We're just going through a transition phase. The nature of the changes that have taken place in this century – I mean, goodness me, the whole century's been a transition! I'd love to be around long enough to see what the next century is going to turn out like. It's going to be more of a consolidating period, isn't it? It has to be, because so many of the revolutions in world history have taken place in the last one hundred and fifty years.

A while back, I heard that the average life expectancy of a man who retires at the age of sixty is fourteen years, and the average life expectancy of a man who retires at sixty-five is fourteen months. That may have changed since then, but the fact is that we often ask people to do the biggest, most demanding projects in their last five years of their working lives.

My father died at sixty-four, before he retired. He was deputy general manager of the Savings Bank, and they put him in charge of the computerisation of all the bank's branches. But he was an old copperplate accountant and he just couldn't cope. He had two or three heart attacks in a week and was gone. I mean, it must have been work, because he was waking up in the middle of the night seeing flashing lights. Well, that says 'computers' to me. So, we probably place far too much of a burden on people in those last years before retirement.

It's not so bad for bishops because they're generally in the role for some time, so it doesn't change. I mean, I've been

Archbishop since 1991, so I'm fairly familiar with the role now, and for me to go on for another five years is not a great burden. In fact, there are so many things that we're just beginning to get going, which I really want to see consolidated, so I need that five years.

I do exercises every day – well almost every day, depending on how rushed I am. I do the old Canadian Airforce 5BXs, and I've been doing them for, oh, thirty-five years. They were developed for men and women in the Canadian Airforce, and it's a graduated scale. Now, I've never aspired to reach the aircrew level, but I do the standard exercises as a self-defence mechanism; it enables me to eat and drink what I like and I don't put on weight. I can still wear the same clothes, but I wouldn't claim to be enormously fit.

It does give the heart a work-out, which you're supposed to do every day. Well, I also drink a good deal of red wine, which you're supposed to do to keep your heart in good condition. I don't do that every day, but I do it with regularity! I've got an uncle who is now ninety-seven, and who still has most of his marbles. Quite remarkable! I can only put it down to stress that killed my father, because he didn't smoke, he had regular exercise, he wasn't overweight, and we all have low blood pressure, which is supposed to be an asset. So, it's really quite perplexing, and I've never quite worked that one out. I tell you what though, I was rather relieved when I passed my father's age!

But I think we really ought to encourage some people to retire early. There's no question in my mind that some of our clergy, for example, actually run down. They burn out, and they really ought to be encouraged to retire at fifty-five or sixty, and if they want to do voluntary stuff in the church, great!

I also think people should retire when they feel they're

ready to retire. I mean, there's enormous wastage in the community, which we can no longer afford in South Australia as the average age of our population goes up. We can't expect all the young people to be supporting all these ageing and aged people. I know a lot of young people who say, 'Oh well, the more people who retire, the more opportunities there are for good jobs,' and that's true, but the community hasn't yet geared itself to effectively use the talents of retired people.

I used to do the art critiques for the *News*. I started while I was a lawyer and then, in New York, I actually did my thesis on 'the aesthetic experience and the religious experience: the links between art and religion'. As soon as I came back from the US, the *News* asked me to take it on again, and I did that for a number of years, including when I was in Woomera, which involved too much travel. My family probably suffered – same old story.

Art is really very close to my heart, and the first thing that I want to do when I retire is to actually finish the book that I've been writing for the last thirty years on the Church and the arts. When I first did my thesis, McGraw Hill was going to publish it, but I didn't have time to re-write it for publication. It would have been one of the first in the field. Now hundreds or thousands of people have been there and into it, so it's nothing new, but I think I've got a few things to say that are a bit new.

I've had lots of artist friends and I still open two or three exhibitions a year, which makes me do some homework and spend some time with the artist. That's all great fun, you know, so I find that very refreshing.

When I'm travelling for meetings or such, I get a few hours in to visit museums of art. My wife says I'm a museum collector! I used to know where every picture was in a lot of different museums. Of course, being in New York, and doing a thesis on art, gave me the excuse to spend one day a week in the galleries. So I knew the Museum of Modern Art and Metropolitan Museum like the back of my hand, and a lot of the commercial galleries too. I wish I'd made more effort to meet the artists, but I met a few of them, and now they're household names.

Pretty much all of my travel is involved with my position. I can't afford to travel unless somebody else pays. I was incredibly lucky to be able to go to New York to study, as that meant I could have time in Europe on the way, and my wife and I spent six months in Europe on the way home, going to Israel as well. Since then I've been very lucky, visiting many places around the globe on Church business. There are lots of places I'd still love to go, but I've been very, very lucky.

I think that the way a Christian approaches ageing must be different from a non-Christian. I mean, in a sense, coming from a Christian perspective, everything's in God's hands anyway. Whether you die today or tomorrow is His business. As far as we're concerned, it's irrelevant. He's in charge.

Also, for a Christian, death and dying is, (although I know a lot of Christians who don't agree with this) in a sense, something to be embraced and looked forward to. I mean, I don't see this world like the old Puritans used to, as the Vale of Tears and the Valley of Testing and all that stuff. I think this world is fantastic. It's God's world and it's so full of amazing things, there's so much joy – and pain too of course that goes with it. But I mean that I want to know what's on the other side. Don't you? And I'm not afraid of it.

One of my theology professors used to say, 'Heaven is an unlimited supply of ice-cream and strawberries!' In other words, heaven is the absolute fulfilment of our deepest desires.

Now, I'm not so sure about that. It's very interesting to me that Jesus taught us almost nothing about heaven, or what follows this life. I'm sure that's no accident; we weren't meant to know.

I don't speculate about it really, but as a matter of logic (and of course God's logic is not necessarily the same as ours) you'd *have* to believe that heaven is something about the harmonious resolution of all conflicts, the forgiveness of all wrongs, the coming together of all people, and the joy of fulfilment.

My understandings have broadened over the years, and they've opened like a flower – that's a bit soapy, and I'm sure a good poet could do much better than that, but there's a sense in which every experience and every human encounter enriches you. Something rubs off, even in a bad encounter, which becomes part of you, and something of you rubs off on others. It's a constant pushing of the frontiers, of the borders.

Art is a classic example. You go into a gallery and you hear people say, 'Oh, my kids could've done that, or done better than that.' Or: 'Can't stand that. What junk! How dare they hang that rubbish on the wall!' Every piece of art is an offering that calls from us a response, yet we're not always willing to respond, because sometimes it challenges at such a level that we can't cope, and so we move on.

John Olsen, the painter, has this wonderful phrase: 'The vital importance of discourse.' If you're prepared to engage in a discourse, in a conversation with the artist, something of what the artist has to offer comes in to you and you change in the process. It's the same with life, if you're prepared to embrace experiences, people and so on, inevitably your world just becomes bigger and bigger and bigger. The really sad people are those people whose worlds become smaller and smaller, as they get older.

My Mum had Alzheimer's Disease for ten years, so we saw her go through this terribly sad diminution in which her world eventually became one room. She only lived in that one room in the house, and it was only then that we discovered what was the trouble. But that's a particular condition. You don't have to have Alzheimer's, do you, for your world to become smaller and smaller, less and less? There's something about Jesus' teaching which is very, very germane to all this, you know, when he talks about love.

When we first are born, we can only relate to mother, and then we gradually learn to relate to the 'old man' about eight, nine months down the track. Then we gradually begin to relate to siblings, and then we get old enough to go to school and relate to a broader group. As we get older we meet more groups. It seems to me that Jesus was the one human being who was capable of relating, at depth and effectively, to every single human being he met.

Now, you or I can't do this, because we're afraid, and we have defence mechanisms, and we have reservations. Unless it's someone who's so extraordinarily outgoing that they get under our guard immediately, we take a little time but gradually we open up as we learn to trust them and to have confidence in them. We can be real with them, but only with a limited number of people. I mean how many close friends do any of us have with whom we can really be totally open? It seems to me that there's a magnificent model in Jesus there, which is a constant challenge to us in terms of letting our experience open us up all the time.

As you age, I think it is important to first of all focus on what kind of person you think you really are, and ask yourself if you are living that, because if you are, you're going to be a fulfilled person. I'd like to say. 'What kind of person do you think God has made you, and are you living that?' And, 'Does God have a significant role in your life that gives you purpose and meaning and forgiveness and encouragement and love and the Spirit?' I mean, that's the evangelistic message.

But also, I think most men in our society are pretty driven, and most are still pretty well dominated by their parents' expectations of them, and other people's expectations. You know, the really mature person learns to recognise those expectations by the time they're fifty, and starts to do something about them. Some of us go through the whole of our lives still being dominated and controlled by some of those expectations, but we at least need to make the effort to look at them.

I have a very good friend, who's a psychiatrist, and he says that we all have these little tapes in the back of our minds that our parents, our schoolteachers and various other people have programmed into us. Until we recognise those tapes and destroy them, we're not ourselves; we're still being dominated by others' expectations.

I think one of the problems of ageing is that none of us really ever think we're old. I mean, we're still the same kids we were at fifteen, and twenty-six, or thirty-five or fifty. I think that means we fool ourselves. I mean, we're great at denying what is happening to us, both within and without, so that probably prevents a lot of us taking the process of ageing seriously. I can't do the pull-ups on the beam that I used to be able to do, but I can still do the press-ups. As I said earlier, I find that I can function effectively for a long period if I have a siesta, which gives me a break. But we're still the same people at heart, aren't we?

I read an enormous amount of poetry. I love poetry. I try and write some occasionally, but it's pretty inferior stuff. I don't think I could dignify myself by saying I'm a poet, but I am of a poetic kind. I mean, I appreciate playing with the language, which is what a poet does, and I suppose that by virtue of my theological and legal training, I'm a word man. But my heart is in the visual, and if I really had had the time, I would like to have developed my capacity to articulate visual images much more effectively. The life expectancy these days is between seventy-five and eighty, and if I get a decade after I retire and can really work hard at this, I might develop something.

One of the things I'm learning is that it's high time to find a little more time for me. It's time for me to be doing a few more of the things that I really enjoy doing. That doesn't necessarily mean that it's not work related, but I've been so driven and such a workaholic for thirty-five years of ordained ministry, that more often than not I've had to say, 'No, I can't do that, as I've got to do this.' The list of priorities is long, and down the bottom somewhere, I'll get to some of the things that I really want to do.

This is why I'm enjoying painting one day a month, you see. However, my technical skills are nowhere near my history or philosophy of art skills, and I always say that 'my aspiration vastly exceeds my perspiration!'

ONE OF THE BOYS

Bob Watts

Starting out as an apprentice fitter and turner, Bob Watts has had a variety of occupations. There was a stint with Colton, Palmer and Preston, where he did the heat treatment of dies and tooling. Then Bob purchased his own truck and carted sand under government contract. This was followed by trucking for Enfield Council, before moving into landscaping, working first for MF Hodge and Sons, where he was in charge of the Landscape Department. For fifteen years before retirement, Bob was curator of the Levels Campus of the South Australian Institute of Technology, a position gained when the campus was first established. Over the years, Bob has been actively involved with several sporting organisations, including the West Torrens Baseball Club, Port Adelaide Baseball Club, and the previous West Torrens Football Club, where he was a committee member. Now he's an active golfer and a member of a fitness group.

We photographed Bob after his early morning swim at Henley Beach with the Grunters, then interviewed him at his well-maintained suburban home.

Right through the year, early in the morning, I go down to the Henley Surf Lifesaving Club with the 'Grunters'. We go three days a week – Monday, Wednesday and Friday. If the weather's suitable, we go swimming, but there's a real good gym down there, so we do exercises. There's a rowing machine, bench machines, weights, and all the rest of it. We're associate members of the Henley Surf Club.

We used to be members over at the Thebarton Oval, using the gym there. It really started with a fellow called Grinter, who was a footballer for West Torrens. He reckoned that half us fellows over there were fat and useless, so he got us all together. We were all West Torrens Football Club members, some were past players, and we'd meet at the Club for a drink. Then we decided on this fitness group and called it 'Grinter's Grunters'. That was about eighteen years ago, and now we are just the 'Grunters'. We don't know where Grinter is these days. Last year we got all the boys together for a reunion, and rang all over Australia, but couldn't find him.

When West Torrens, known as the Eagles, joined with Woodville Football Club, and our club was going to be sold, one of the other fellows said, 'Why don't you join down at Henley?' He was a member of the Lifesaving Club. Henley's better anyway, because it's close to the beach.

Your health is a funny thing. Some days you go down there and you can get on the rowing machine and you might row two thousand metres. Other mornings, you might only row a thousand because – this is what I think anyway, I could be wrong – at times your body goes up, hits a high and then goes down, just like a graph. If you are down, it's silly to push yourself too hard. Some mornings when I go down there, I feel good and exercising is easy, but if I'm a bit lethargic, or off-colour, I take it easy.

If the weather is too miserable, we don't swim, but we've got the sauna down there, and we just work out in the gym. Some of them go for a walk, but I don't walk much now. I used to go running and that, but I had both hips replaced about six years ago. There is a fellow who played in my baseball team years ago, and now he's a doctor, and he said to me, 'Give that running away.'

I had one hip done in October that year, but Bett and I wanted to go overseas, and the other hip started to play up. So I went back and I said to him, 'Look, I don't know, but we want to go over to England in March, and I think we'll have to cancel because it's just too sore.' He said, 'Oh!' Anyway he looked up in his book, and he said, 'We'll do it in January for you.' So, he did the other one. It was a piece of cake, it really was. I'd have it done again tomorrow!

What finally decided me to have the hips done was that we, the Grunters, had a ten-day trip to Hawaii. It was real good – just the fellows! We used to go dancing at the night-clubs and that, but I got so that I could hardly walk home, so that decided me. As long as I was laying flat somewhere I was alright, but as soon as I got up, the pain was there again. It's the best thing I ever did, and I've not had trouble since, except sometimes when you get into a position, like if you go to pick a weed up, or you stretch over somewhere, you might have to get up, stand up and then get going again.

The Grunters are a varied group. One fellow works for a stock journal, another is in charge of fundraising for Surf Lifesaving. One is in charge of spare parts, another is manager for a tube manufacturing company, others are a motor mechanic, bar manager, and a surveyor. The youngest would be fifty-five and I'm seventy-five, so I'm the oldest.

There were about, I think, twenty of us when we first

started up, but now there's about eight of us. We don't really have new fellows, as look, it's hard to get the right people to join, because you don't want any arguments, you don't want any 'blues', and all the rest of it. I mean, we've been together that long now that as soon as somebody walks in, you know if he's in a good mood or a bad mood, and if it's bad, you tend to leave him alone. You know what I mean? I don't know what women are like, but men, you can tell one another exactly what you think of them and say, you know, 'Just ease up.' Well, we've had no problems, and we haven't had any trouble at all.

The Grunters have had a few shows, but we're fairly quiet now, I suppose. We don't do a great deal. We don't go out much of a night-time because if you have three or four or five schooners, or whatever, and drive home, you're likely to have to blow in the bag on the way, and this, to me, has ruined everything. Look, I'm not a drunk, but I like my beer. The other day, I went with some golfing mates up to Innamincka, and about thirty miles the other side of Leigh Creek, there was a breathalyser on the road. Now, you'd die of thirst out there, but he pulled us over and said, 'Would you blow in the bag?' You have got to be joking!

I'm a member of the Westward Ho Golf Club. I play there every Thursday, and then about once a fortnight with the South Australian Metropolitan Fire Service Golf Club. A great friend of mine, who used to live around on the next street, was a station officer in the fire brigade, and I used to get him to come and help me where I worked at landscaping, if I was busy. Then I got to know three or four others, and if I got extra busy, I'd get them to help. So that's how come I'm an associate member of the Fire Service Golf Club.

Soon we're going up to Swan Hill to play Victoria, which

we do each year. We've been to Innamincka, out in the middle of nowhere, to play golf. That was excellent. They just put a stick in the middle of the donga and you hit up to that. We had a great time. Just us fellows, as we don't let the girls on these trips. It's too rough! When we play the annual Australian Fire Service Golf Championships, the girls do go then because while we're playing golf, the girls are looked after, taken on tours and whatever. When the golf finishes, we all meet back at the club, have a drink, and then go to the shows afterwards. We go to a different capital city every year.

Being a fitter and turner, there are lots of things around to keep me busy. I've still got my own welding gear and all the tools of the trade. I use them just about all the time. With the lads from the golf club, their buggies fall to bits, so they'll bring it down and I'll weld that up for them. Once they know that you've got this gear, everybody asks you to do things. I mean, the fellow next-door breaks a rake handle, or something comes off his car, or something wants welding, and you know, it just keeps you busy and out of bother.

If I'm home, I still work fairly hard. I do the 'outside'. There is a big backyard. We've got cabbages, caulies, tomatoes, cucumbers, beans and spuds. I don't fuss around with them much, and if they don't grow, they don't grow. I've got a sprinkler system down the side for the camellias, and I've just got to turn on a couple of valves. Same out the front, as that's all irrigated.

Tell you what, I don't mind cooking. I think it's good. I don't like any fancy food. I like plain food. I don't like pasta because, to me, pasta's a lot of wriggly things you put on a plate and cover with sauce, and if you didn't cover it with sauce you couldn't eat it. I think it's tasteless. So, I like roasts, fish, steak, and barbecues.

People eat too much. Some guys are enormous. Some of them haven't seen their feet for years, but if that's the way they want to live, I don't care what they do. I don't have lunch. I'll have breakfast, maybe a sausage, a couple of eggs, tomato, and a couple of slices of toast, but I'll have nothing during the day. I enjoy my tea of a night-time.

My health is excellent, and I think it's what you eat. I'm lucky because I like salads, cold meat, cheese, and I love bread. I wouldn't care if all the chocolate factories burnt down. Look, I'm not saying that I don't like chocolate, but I just won't eat it, because I get stubborn I suppose.

I weighed thirteen-and-a-half stone when we first got married and we were living down at Largs Bay. I looked at myself and I thought, 'This is grotesque.' But I've been eleven-and-a-half stone now for thirty or forty-odd years. If I start to get a bit of a pudding on me, I don't eat so much, or I go and do a bit more work, or some more sit-ups, and it doesn't take much to get it off. And yet I eat what I want to eat.

Being active, that's the main thing. Keep moving, although some days you don't feel like it. I mean it's no good saying, 'Don't do this, and don't do that,' and, 'Get out and walk,' as a lot of people can't walk, or aren't able to get out and exercise. But I still think a lot of them could do more than what they're doing. I think they can get off their bum of a morning and do something, even if it's just laying on the floor and stretching.

I don't walk a lot. I've got a gammy knee and I had the cartilage out, so the bone's rubbing on bone there. But I ride a little bike around the golf course, mainly because I can't see the point in wearing my hips out!

Also, one of the main things is that you've got to be lucky, and I'm lucky that I've had good health. Now, whether that's because of what I've done, or because of my build, my metabolism or whatever, I wouldn't have a clue. Some people are big and they're going to stay big I suppose, but they don't have to get bigger. This is what annoys me, but then I don't say anything, because it's got nothing to do with me.

I played baseball from when I was about seventeen until I was fifty-three. Two of the lads that I served my apprenticeship with were baseballers. They were my friends, so naturally I went and played baseball with them, which was good. We won a few premierships. I was the president, chairman and so forth of the baseball club for years. I'm also a life member. I had fun with them. We used to have parties and that, but with all the parties we had, not once did anyone step out of line. We used to have some fancy dress parties that'd just about turn your ear, but straight down the middle, you know.

I think people can stay with clubs too long. It's not that you're not wanted, but people grow up and go past you, do you know what I mean? Their ideas are different.

I've always been that way that I don't care what anybody else does, and as long as they don't try and tell me what to do, I don't try and tell them. Same as with our two lads, I don't care what they do. I told them when they first got married, 'If I can help you, I'll help you, but I'm not going to tell you what to do.' If they want to, they can come and ask, that's different, and we get on pretty well. One lad is in Alice Springs and the other is down here.

There are five grandchildren. I suppose I'm a bit grumpy at times with them. I won't stand any messing around. I mean, it was the same with our two lads. If I told them to do something, and they didn't do it, they were in trouble. But the grandchildren come down here, and they know what the rules are, and no problem! I think I get on as well with them as anybody. We go and have a game of cricket, or go down the beach or something. They're alright. They're good. The other two grandchildren are in Alice Springs and we go up there quite often to see them, probably once a year.

We used to drive up to Alice Springs, but Bett said the last time we went that she wouldn't drive up again, as it's too far, but I love driving. About the only place we haven't seen in Australia would be up around Broome. We've been up to Kununurra, staying for a week on each of three stations, camping out under the stars every night. That was excellent. Even when we were young, we'd chuck the kids in, take the trailer and an army tent, and go camping. They were some of the best times with the kids.

I've got a 1975 Holden Premier, top of the line, and it's only done sixty-eight thousand kilometres. Brand spanking new, virtually. Beautiful car. I've only had it about a year and a half. It used to belong to a mate of my father's, and when this fellow died, his daughter said to me, 'Look, would you like to buy Dad's car?' Because I hadn't seen it for years I said, 'Why, what's it like?' As soon as I saw it I said, 'Yeah, I'll have that.' It's magnificent. It's only had two sets of tyres on it. It's not even run in!

We've driven around overseas too. I didn't like England much, it's all stacked up, but once you get out of the cities, lovely. London itself, I wouldn't give you two bob for, but Wales was beautiful, and I loved Scotland. We went to Canada and then flew down to do a tour down through the Rockies, down through Denver into Colorado. That's about the prettiest I've seen. Absolutely out of this world. Beautiful. I'd go back there tomorrow.

I went to Bali with the Grunters, about three years ago, and that was a real good trip. We went up right in the middle of the mountains, then we came down in these boats, white water rafting. Bett and I have been to Bali twice too, and we've been to New Zealand and Tasmania. I can't see the point of people working all their lives and saving and not using what they've worked for. I'm on super, not a big super, but we get by and we don't want for anything. When we retired, the guy that we went and saw said, 'Look, scrape the cream off the top every year and use it.' That's what we've done.

Although I started out as a fitter and turner, after other jobs, including trucking, I moved into landscaping. A good friend of mine who played in my baseball side used to get a few jobs with a landscaping business, and he said to me, 'Will you give us a hand with some of these gardens?' He taught me pruning and so forth, and I was there to put in a few lawns and do a few jobs and all the rest of it. The next minute, I gave the truck away and went gardening because I've always loved gardening, and I like being outside. Well, I don't know any other job where you get as much satisfaction out of putting something in the ground and seeing it grow. It gave me a great deal of pleasure.

Later, I joined MF Hodge and Sons in town and I was in charge of their landscape department for nine years. One of the jobs we did was tennis courts and we levelled the courts for Memorial Drive before they had the Davis Cup. The courts were out three inches down on the sou-western corner. I was amazed. Everybody was, but we levelled that up. We did bowling greens, golf courses, home gardens, and we used to do a lot of country work, a few stations and so forth, putting in irrigation systems and all the rest.

Then a job came up at the Institute of Technology at the Levels Campus. They were just starting off and they wanted a curator out there, so I applied for that and got it, and that was excellent. When I first started, there was nothing, only one building on about a hundred and eighty-odd acres. We put in three ovals, a hockey pitch, soccer ground, and all the gardens, trees, and everything that goes with it. The last thing was putting in the golf course. Toward the finish we had a big staff.

I was there for about fifteen years and I retired when I was fifty-eight. Well, there was nothing else to do; I used to sit in the office and think to myself, 'Now, what'll I do today?' One day I was talking to one of the chaps out there and I said to him, 'They tell me you're going to retire.' He said, 'Yeah,' and I asked, 'Why's that?' He said, 'It's the right time,' and I said, 'Is that right?' Then he said, 'Yeah. You'd better think about it. You got super?' When I said yes, he said, 'Think about it.' So I did, for about four hours, then I went to the girl in the office, she wrote my resignation and I handed it in. Bett just about died with a leg in the air when I told her. Bit of a shock!

The fellow that took over was under me, sort of thing, and straight away he had ideas about what he wanted to do, and that is a good thing. I've driven past there, going up to golf at Gawler a couple of times, and I could see what some-body else had done, and ten out of ten! He could see things that I couldn't see, if you know what I mean? I had been out there too long. Time to go.

Being retired is good because, well, you can please your-self. You don't have to get up and do this or that, although it comes back to routine again. I mean, as soon as the paper hits the ground of a morning I've got to get up and go and have a look at it. I don't go to bed before half past ten, quarter to eleven, and I'm always up around about five.

Getting older though, well, I suppose death is coming round the corner a bit quick, isn't it? But, if it happened tomorrow, I would have no grizzles at all because I've had a good life. There's safety as far as Bett's concerned because, if I happen to peg out, she gets two thirds of our super.

When you are older, the government forgets you. The idea is that when you're retired, you should be able to look after yourself. Well, that's alright if you've got super coming in, but there are thousands of people out there who are not able to look after themselves. I mean, what's going to happen in the future when all these kids now out on the street, who can't get a job, are older. If they can't get a job, they can't get a job. It's no good calling them 'bludgers'. Look, it's like if you've got a sheepdog, and if you don't work the sheepdog, he's going to chase the cat, or pull the towels off the line, or something else. It's got to be worked!

I was fortunate, I left school at Thebie Tech on the Friday, and I started work on the Monday. Also, in those days, the local copper'd tell you, 'If I catch you riding your bike again without a light, you're in trouble,' and he'd give you a boot up the backside. If you went and told your dad, he would give you another one. But they weren't cruel. You'd go to school and you knew you're going to get a belting if you did something wrong. There was no good grizzling about it, and you put your hands out and copped it. These days, everybody's got an excuse.

You don't need a great deal of money as you get older. It's nice to have it, I suppose, and it would be great if I could win a couple hundred thousand. Nothing would give me greater pleasure than to pick up the phone and say to the two lads, 'Eh, you'd better come down and see us.' I'd give them half.

Then I'd catch the first plane out. I wouldn't care where I was going, but I'd love to go to America again, down through New Mexico. I'd like to get on the bus, see something, say, 'This isn't bad,' get off the bus, have a look around, and stay there for a time. Cities don't do anything for me, but just to get on the bus again and just go, that'd suit me right down to the ground.

Honestly, I don't feel any different now than what I did since I can't remember when. I don't feel any different. I don't feel as though there's anything I can't do. As I say, I can't run as fast, and all the rest of it, and I don't try, but I can play golf. I don't feel as if there's anything different, and I don't feel much different in myself.

We get around all over. A friend used to have a mine at Andamooka, so we've been up there quite often opal mining. That was good fun, but he has since died. They were real great times. I love fishing. We go out to Point Turton, on the Peninsula. Last time the Grunters went out there we hired two boats and went out about thirteen or fourteen mile. We got a mixed bag, including a shark that'd be, I suppose, about six foot. Gutted that and there was beautiful flesh on that. Excellent. But if I can get fresh tommies, I'll have fresh tommies. To me, tommies have got more taste than any other fish.

I used to love dancing. When I was young, I used to go dancing three nights a week up to the Embassy, the Palais, and Palladium, and we used to have a real good time. But in those days, even the girls could safely walk anywhere. It was a totally different world. Anyhow, there was a great big hall, seventy yards long. Everyone would be going like blazes down one side of the hall – four and five hundred people dancing! Tuesday night used to be a 'swing night'. It was good fun.

In life, I've been very, very fortunate, I must say. As a kid, I don't know whether they tried to get me out of the house or not, but I always seemed to finish up at Melrose at my grandma's and my uncle's place. Uncle had a trucking business up there in the Lower Flinders. I've been all over Mount Remarkable, and up the top there, shooting rabbits and foxes. A packet of fifty 22 long rifle bullets cost six shillings a box.

When I was about ten or eleven, I went to Wilpena Pound with my uncle, and it took us two days. That was years ago and there was nothing there except the station. I can remember that we went to the Wilmington Pub. He wasn't a big drinker, my uncle, but a hell of a nice guy, and he said, 'Come on and I'll buy you a drink.' We went into the Wilmington Pub and he bought me a pint of sarsaparilla. That was the first drink in a pub I had.

I think that one of the bad things on this earth is TV. It brainwashes the young people! If I had kids again, the kids would watch it for an hour a day, and no more. They come home from school and sit straight in front of the television. To me, that's not on. I do watch it, but mostly SBS because there's no ads. I've usually got a book, a murder mystery or something, and if there's nothing on, I'll flick the TV off and read.

I'll watch footy on the TV, but I'm not too wrapped up in cricket. I reckon some of them are cheats, and those jokers should have been rubbed out for taking that money. They know what's right and what's wrong. The rules are there and they know what they are. They only got a little smack on the wrist, and that turns me off. I mean, if they don't want to abide by the rules, don't make them. It's just not on. This is why I like golf. There was a player the other day who marked his ball and made a mistake when he picked it up. Then he called the referee over and told the referee what he did, and he automatically dropped a stroke. Now, he didn't have to say anything, but if you play golf, you're the one who hits the balls, and if you cheat, you cheat yourself.

As you get older, you learn more. I mean, I'm surprised at

times about what people do, and I think to myself, 'What did you do that for?' They can't see the hole in the fence, if you know what I mean. But as I say, you can't tell other people what to do, and I think once you start telling somebody what to do, that is when you get into trouble.

I'm an atheist. I don't believe in religion. I just can't understand it. I mean, we talk about this at times. 'Well, I've never seen God and none of you jokers have.' And I said, 'And tell me where hell is?' And they don't know. I said, 'Where's heaven?' They don't know. And I said, 'It's a load of garbage as far as I'm concerned.' There's only one thing I believe in, and that's what we've got here, my family and the kids and the grandkids and all the rest of it. And what's more, most of the wars have been because of religion.

I've been married for years, but I don't know the date. Dates, to me, mean nothing – not a thing. There's a little card on the side of the fridge with all the kid's birthdays, but I forget to read that. I can't see the point. I mean, yesterday's gone, tomorrow's coming, and it doesn't alter my thoughts or my feelings about my family or friends.

Bett is a Lavender Lady volunteer at the Royal Adelaide Hospital, and she has got a 'ten-year badge' for that. She does that every Friday. She also belongs to a Probus Club. Now, I could no more join Probus than fly to the moon! It's just not my scene, you know. Same as bowls. I couldn't play bowls. That would drive me up the wall. After about three innings, they go and have a cup of tea, and then they come out and bowl again. Oh no!

Well, I think you only own one thing in your life, and that's what's in your skin and your body. If you want to stuff it up, you stuff it up. I reckon something tells you if you're going wrong, and I think your body gets used to doing a certain thing all the time, such as when you eat. You get used to doing certain things.

I just think you've got to do what you want to do, as long as you don't hurt people, and if you can do it, go and do it, because you never know what's around the corner. I could be wrong, but that's what my thoughts are!

NOT TO YIELD

Don McDonald

As a member of the 1987 Steering Committee for the University of the Third Age (U3A) in South Australia, and later as a tutor, Don McDonald has facilitated opportunities for retired people to learn about subjects that are of interest to them. At the age of eighty-five, he remains committed to the U3A, and continues to teach a course called 'Words Alive!' Initially a primary school teacher in 1931, Don later became a teacher of Latin and English at Adelaide High School before moving to the country to teach at Gawler and Mt Gambier. He was the principal of high schools at Minlaton, Millicent, Murray Bridge, and Elizabeth. Over the years, Don has enjoyed conducting choirs, as he does at the retirement village in which he now lives. Don's wife, Bertha, is a resident at a nursing home in a nearby suburb. Don has been awarded Life Membership of the U3A in Tea Tree Gully, and in recent years, has been a nominated finalist for the Arthur Cys Medal for Outstanding Service to Seniors (Council on the Ageing), and for Senior Citizen of the Year (Tea Tree Gully).

Don's interview took place in the front room of his neat open-plan home unit, part of a modern retirement village, set well back from a main road in an Adelaide suburb.

I am trying to recall that far-off first day of retirement. It was the day I stepped out of the most rewarding period of my professional career. Looking ahead to that day, one of my conflicting thoughts had been, 'Now I march to my own drum.' But even from the first day, there was another feeling – a feeling, if you like, of being adrift, or of having closed the door on a room full of people and noise and action. Of course, the rhythm of life took over again and new harmonies emerged. After all, I'd retired not to escape but to seek new horizons.

At present, almost a quarter of a century on, my major activities are reduced to two or three – but they are of a satisfying richness.

Generally, I visit my wife in the nursing home twice a day. I help her every evening with her meal. Her stroke in 1997 knocked out a number of brain cells and so she is blind. She's had several strokes. After an earlier stroke, when she temporarily lost some of her sight, her reaction when I visited her the next day in hospital was, in a tone of tragedy, 'I can't see!' The interesting thing is that now, when she's totally blind, or so nearly that it doesn't matter, no worries! It's not a thing that seems to be on her mind at all.

I read to her and, you know, do things that are designed to help her brain wake up. In the beginning I read an account that I wrote about our travels in the Centre of Australia. I had called it 'Cruising in the Centre', as we had a Land Cruiser. Reading that was good because, although her memory is shot to pieces, the discussion that followed the reading of a particular incident stimulated her memory, though she mightn't remember it on the next visit.

Well, we did the same thing with her own typed account of 'Impressions of an Overseas Trip'. In 1979 we travelled widely in the UK and Europe and she wrote it up. So, I was reading bits of that to her, and it did the same trick. I've read all sorts of things to her recently, for example Colin Thiele's latest book, *With Dew on My Boots*. That was stimulating as Bertha and I both knew Colin, and found in his book echoes of our lives in the thirties.

I came across a slim little book, *La Dernière Classe*, which I had read at school, and as Bertha was good at French when she was at school, I've been reading little bits of that to her. I said, 'This is *La Dernière Classe*.' And she said, 'The Last Class.' That has interesting implications about her memory. I read the book phrase by phrase in French and then I translate it into English, just pausing to see if she's twittering with a translation, and often it comes. That has been a useful and most interesting process. You'd think it might be rather tedious, but she has, in fact, quite enjoyed it.

Now, going back a little further, about a year ago we couldn't get her to say her name, so we'd make a little game of it. 'Come on, what is your name?' No response. Well, eventually we'd get to 'Bertha McDonald'. Then, one day we went through the routine again, and I said, 'Come on, what is your name?' '*Je ne sais pas*.' In French that means 'I don't know.' Says something about the human brain, doesn't it?

And that's the way we go on. Then, there's music. I play tape recordings of familiar music for her. Bertha was a very fine musician, a good pianist and a singing teacher. She and I were involved in choral societies. When we went to Mount Gambier in 1947, Bertha became the pianist of the junior and senior Choral Societies, and I became the conductor of the juniors.

Bertha has been in nursing homes since February 1997. First of all she was hospitalised for assessment and placed temporarily in a nursing home. Then we had the amazing good fortune for her to be permanently placed in the best nursing home anywhere within reach of the retirement village. My daughter, son and I all feel very fortunate that such a pleasant place was available for her.

I've easily adjusted to living on my own. For maybe ten years now, I've been doing most of the cooking, most of the housework. The main change was being on my own instead of having her company, as we have been together for a long time. We celebrate our sixtieth wedding anniversary in May this year. In other ways though, it was a relief from the burden of care. After her first stroke she came back home again. The Royal District Nursing Service nurses visited, but it was particularly a strain at night when she tended to get out of bed, you know, just half-awake. Instead of sitting in my den I sat near the bedroom so that I could keep an eye on that door.

I don't have a lot of other activities now, because visiting Bertha, cooking, and doing all the usual things that one does about the house and garden, means that my time is fragmented.

However, there's the University of the Third Age – U3A. That is my second major activity. It involves one session a fortnight and preparation. I first became involved with U3A in 1986. There was an advertisement in the paper describing this fairly new movement which originated in France, Toulouse actually, and anyone interested was invited to a meeting. I was interested because two of my cousins had helped establish the U3A in Melbourne. I was one of the volunteers, and I became a member of the Steering Committee in Adelaide.

A few months later I started teaching at Tea Tree Gully. Being a member of a committee trying to establish a baby organisation, you are trying desperately to find people who are willing to take part in it, and you feel you've got to volunteer yourself. So, what could I do? I volunteered to take a class in, well, let's call it public speaking with a special interest in words, in language. That developed into what I now call 'Words Alive!', and I'm now in my thirteenth year of tutoring that class.

My subtitle for the course is 'Language Awareness'. It is not so much a course as an adventure in language awareness, including the use of language, and the history and roots of the English language. Words have a life of their own. They reproduce, proliferate, degenerate, become tyrants or invaluable servants. Particularly, we observe changes in usage over the years, note the growing role of English as a global language, and we focus on the nature of language and its role in human relationships. A multitude of topics flood in on us as the year goes on. We aim to 'light fires of curiosity about the central human characteristic of language'.

Each session closes with what I call 'a spot o' guid stuff', which is simply a verse or whatever, that might be worth hearing for its own sake. My Scottish ancestry sometimes influences my choice! What I read to the class yesterday was a little poem called 'A Kiss of the King's Hand'. It is presented as the tender memory of a lass who kissed Bonnie Prince Charlie's weary, battle-stained hand as she farewelled him on the sea-shore; so honoured that she 'durstna raise her een'. Simple, moving words – in line with my aim to focus on language in use.

What drives me in this is a love of the language, and it's a joy trying to impart it. I was an English teacher, and my present fascination with the language must have begun there. That passion was stimulated not only by the students that I taught, and their often perceptive responses, but also by some marvellous colleagues with whom I was associated.

Sure, I wouldn't be teaching the class at U3A if I didn't derive pleasure from doing so. Apparently the people who come are satisfied. I marvel sometimes that some of them have been coming for four, five, or six years. They claim that I don't seem to repeat myself, but I do, and each repetition brings in something new, to me as well as to my friends. It's a poor teacher who doesn't learn.

And there's much to learn from the members of the class. They're such a mix: at the moment a couple of pharmacists, a director of nursing, a German airman and his wife, a lady from Bulgaria (recently naturalised and teaching migrant children in local schools), a lecturer on Ancient Egypt – and so on and on, not forgetting the lady from Malta, from whom we gain lots of little details about the Maltese language and history, and many perceptive comments about learning English.

There are twenty-three on my roll at present. People can join at any time during the year because it's not a sequential course. Each topic is complete in itself, but I hope that they all connect up in our computer brains and become systematised, with a little aid from the tutor.

At the U3A Tea Tree Gully, we offer, I suppose, about thirty different subjects, including various languages, computing, painting, philosophy, health promotion, legal studies – the range is ever growing and it caters for many different tastes. Not everyone wants to go into the subject at great depth, and one of the attractions is that there is no examination at the end of it. Many people just feel, 'I've always wanted to learn about that, and now's my chance.'

Our philosophy is foreshadowed in Tennyson's 'Ulysses'. We could do worse than take the last few lines as a motto. During the poem Ulysses is pictured as saying:

> *I cannot rest from travel: I will drink*
> *Life to the lees: all times I have enjoy'd*
> *Greatly, have suffer'd greatly, both with those*
> *That loved me, and alone; on shore, and when*
> *Thro' scudding drifts the rainy Hyades*
> *Vext the dim sea: I am become a name;*

and . . .

> *Yet all experience is an arch wherethro'*
> *Gleams that untravell'd world whose margin fades*
> *For ever and for ever when I move.*

and . . .

> *Tho' much is taken, much abides; and tho'*
> *We are not now that strength which in old days*
> *Moved earth and heaven; that which we are, we are;*
> *One equal temper of heroic hearts,*
> *Made weak by time and fate, but strong in will*
> *To strive, to seek, to find, and not to yield.*

You can't stop. That's life. Life-long learning is the goal, and we might just as well be doing it in a more or less systematic way. So now we follow up the avenues that particularly appeal to us, or that we would have liked to follow in other times, but were restricted by the demands of employment. Yes, it's good to be able to march to your own drum! Most of our members seem to be motivated by curiosity, by a thirst for knowledge of one kind or another.

However, there's more to it than slaking that thirst. You meet such a lot of people with richly varying personalities who open your eyes to other attitudes and interests. There's a great deal of camaraderie and absorption of various cultures, simply through association with each other. For example, in the middle of the year we have a special winter Christmas Carol session. Some of our members brought recordings of carols from different countries, so there was cross-cultural influence.

During the first year of U3A at Tea Tree Gully, when trying to persuade people to take part as tutors, I said to my friend, the late Fred Champion, also a retired headmaster, 'What about it Fred?' He said, 'I don't know, but I could offer you a course in caravanning in remote areas.' I said, 'Done!' He became more and more enthusiastic about that, and the result was that we had a dozen or so people keenly involved in caravanning in the outback. We couldn't keep him though. In 1991 Fred, at age seventy-five, led a group re-enacting Edward John Eyre's crossing of the Great Australian Bight! There's a leader for you – the sort you love to attract to U3A, even if only for a one-off course. Such was one of the tutors in astronomy, a well-known discoverer of comets! We are as happy to enlist inspired, enthusiastic amateurs, as to be led by retired professionals.

Bertha and I have done a lot of travelling in Australia, seizing every opportunity to explore and savour the outback. We'd always loved camping, and never a year went by without some camping holiday. On retirement we were happy to repeat the established patterns – with more happy gatherings around camp-fires (with four grandchildren and their parents, and occasional 'camp-followers'): more sing-songs led by our son with his guitar and his repertoire of colonial songs.

Frequently we'd pass through Moolooloo station (always welcomed, and occasionally guided by the owners), and on to adventures like climbing Mt Patawurta. That sort of thing became an alternative lifestyle for us as we reached the stage where competitive sport was no longer feasible. I had been very keen on tennis, but now that was replaced by activities made possible with our Land Cruiser. We towed a caravan, went fishing, and had memorable adventures. Some were hair-raising enough to tell and retell in later years. Some of my friends say I've reached my anecdotage!

The music, the grandeur and solitude of the Flinders Ranges – all that 'mighty world of eye and ear' – the companionship of friends, these are harmonies of memories that linger on.

When I was posted to Elizabeth High School in 1969, we purchased a house on an acre of land in the hills near Houghton. From there, I could drive to Elizabeth in twenty minutes. We lived there for twenty-three years, four times as long as we'd lived in any one house. I retired in 1976 when I was sixty-three and the land provided an opportunity to plant trees, grow vegetables, and for me to potter around with carpentry. I renovated the house and added a rumpus room for table tennis. In such ways retirement enabled me to revive old interests and activities.

In moving about from one country house to another, I'd always been involved in practical, do-it-yourself activities around the home. Back in Mt Gambier, in about 1950, when we had to leave our rented house, I built a new one up on the lakeside. I did a lot of the work myself for two reasons – money, and the enjoyment of a new challenge. Working with Mt Gambier limestone, cutting the slabs, and sawing them into 'ashlars' was an experience in itself. If nothing else, it proved that teachers (even English teachers) are not necessarily ignorant of 'the real world'. So that fuelled my interest in practical activities. At the same time, one carried on one's life in the local community.

In the first half a dozen years of living in the hills, I became involved, in a minor way, with some community activities. For example, the people up the road beyond us were short of water. There was agitation, lobbying the government to have a pipeline extended. As one of the locals, I became chairman of a group that was trying to accelerate the government's activity, working to get a storage tank erected at the top of the hill. We enjoyed helping a retired friend and her daughter establish and maintain a hobby farm near Kersbrook.

At this stage, there was plenty to keep me physically active. We acquired an extra acre of land, which led to fencing, tree-planting, gardening and mowing. And there was upkeep – not least the painting of the roof and extensions – like rebuilding the bathroom.

Then, when the Ash Wednesday fires struck, there was an immediate, spontaneous response by the Houghton community. We had a public meeting, and I was elected chairman of a group providing support after the disaster. We did what we could, and the need seemed to have been filled after a few months. Then there was a house fire locally, so we formalised the group to cater for other personal and family emergencies, not necessarily restricted to fires.

The movement, 'A Local Emergency Resource Team' (ALERT), spread. In co-operation with a similar group in Gumeracha, we formed what we called the 'ALERT Central Council' based in Adelaide. Other ALERT groups were formed, and these flourished for a while, both in the city and in southern districts, but they were dependent on the enthusiasm of local people. Fifteen years later, the most active surviving group is at Athelstone, associated with a church group. I didn't seek these activities – they overtook me and carried me along on their crest.

My language skills have been used since retirement in various ways. When we came back from overseas travel, I felt that I was in danger of mental stagnation. There was plenty of physical activity, but I was not doing the things that I had anticipated doing. I hadn't done all the reading I was going to do. I hadn't written anything, and I had ambitions. At that time I spotted an advertisement for people to help as tutors with an Adult Literacy Project, which was a course conducted by TAFE, and designed to train tutors to assist people with language difficulties, particularly literacy.

I applied, and very soon after I was offered a student who happened to be a blind lady living in my vicinity. Doreen had founded a 'Home-makers' Corner' at the Royal Institution for the Blind, and was frustrated at what she felt was her inadequacy at writing reports, chairing meetings, and expressing herself generally. We worked together once a week for about five years. As we worked it first became evident that she wanted to write the story of her pioneering parents, but it soon became clearer that the real story was her own. We worked together on this, but just as we were getting ready to think about publication her husband died; it fell to me to pilot the thing through, until the book was launched. She was honoured in the bicentennial publication *Unsung Heroes and Heroines of Australia*.

Now another opportunity arose. It was to work with a little organisation at Flinders Street Baptist Church. Some enthusiasts had the idea of trying to help migrant women with their language. One of the practical necessities was to look after the children while their mothers were having their lessons, so a Migrant Child Care Centre was established in the church buildings. I was interested in it, with the result that I was invited to take part upstairs teaching English.

My pupil was Chinese, from Penang; she had migrated to

Darwin where she met an Aboriginal lad and they married. My association with her was so enriching for me. I learnt a lot from her, and I got to know her family, mainly through her stories. There was a fascinating story about one of her daughters who, at four years old, suddenly became speechless and withdrawn.

The details of her year of trouble, and its sudden happy ending, have become something like a vicarious memory of my own. I began to understand that I am indeed 'part of all that I have met'. The events and people of her life, as I helped commemorate them in print, began to acquire something of the familiarity of my own personal memories.

And in a different way, that was true of the series of reunions we had in the eighties with people who had been students in Gawler in the forties. Here, surely, is one of the great privileges of a teacher – to be able to meet former students forty years on, to hear how they have battled with life's challenges, and to derive inspiration and encouragement from those students now one's peers. Bertha and I have been admitted to the intimacies of their personal triumphs and tragedies, the successes of their children – even attending a Golden Wedding.

Let's talk about the current phase of my life. We came to the retirement village in 1992, and very soon the people (there are about two hundred) decided they wanted to form a little choir. I became the conductor, and was very involved in the choir for several years.

I'm not a trained musician, but I found great pleasure in conducting, and apparently my lack of professional music qualifications didn't prevent success, in the sense that there was a lot of enjoyment all round. However, I think my greatest musical pleasure has been in performing in local productions of Gilbert & Sullivan opera.

At the beginning of last year, I developed arthritis, particularly in the shoulders. I'd had it years before, commencing when we were touring New Zealand. We had hired a little campervan and it was a bumpy little thing that transmitted all the bumps to the shoulders of the driver. Well, the arthritis went and I'd forgotten all about it, only to be surprised and annoyed when it caught up with me again last year. But here's the good news: thanks to cortisone, expert medical attention, and faithful performance of my stretching exercises – I'm now practically free of it: but I keep my fingers crossed.

Our way of life has always had a dominant spiritual dimension. Bertha's father was a Baptist minister who died at the ripe old age of one hundred, and my father was a local preacher. He and my mother had a very firm Christian faith, and I was brought up in that atmosphere, and still value it. At Mt Gambier and elsewhere I became a local preacher. I still have boxes of sermons that I'd never dare to preach again, as I see my immaturity in some of them! But I know that regardless of the effect on the hearer, the work of preparation was of value to me.

The fact that I don't often attend church now is not a measure of the depth of my Christian faith. I try to do what I think needs to be done within the limits of my capacity, and, I hope, like Telemachus, 'I am decent not to fail in offices of tenderness.'

Although I don't get much time to do so, I love to read. It is 'professional reading' now, preparing for the class that I teach, but I must say that it's still for enjoyment. My shelves are crowded: there's ten years of *English Today*, a quarterly journal; there are penetrating and challenging things such as *The Language Instinct*, and a wide range of general works from *The Man in the Ice* (revealing secrets of the Stone Age) right through to *Walking in the Flinders*, *The Lure of the Limerick* and *Three Men in a Boat*.

I haven't thought much about ageing. For me, blessed with good health, it's a matter of just getting on with life. In any case there's not much you can do about it, except for making the most of what you have left.

I'm very fortunate. I have a lovely family, including a daughter who lives in Aldgate, and who rings me up every night, aware that I'm on my own a lot with no-one to tell about the silly little ordinary trivialities of everyday life. It's nice to natter to her and to our son on Kangaroo Island. I enjoy his weekly phone calls and our chats about the family and the world. We have four grandchildren. I'm looking forward to finding out what it's like to be a great-grandfather, as we have a great-grandson blossoming into a lively two-year-old. They're a lovely family and we are very happy with them all.

I have time for one other regular activity – visiting another retired headmaster who, a year ago, quite suddenly found out that his sight was degenerating. He can still see a little, and he can move around his home, providing no one moves any furniture! He is an inspiration in his cheerful acceptance of his handicap. I visit him now pretty well weekly, to read to him. We share many interests. He's very interested in U3A for example, and in most of the language-related things I'm interested in – Shakespeare particularly. He's a scholarly person and welcomes my modest contributions – even laughs at my jokes.

We also meet twice a year with our former colleagues as Old Headmasters of SA High Schools. The title boils down to the dignified acronym: the OHMS of SAHS – appropriately reminiscent of the GLUGS of GOSH. I remember some years ago when it was announced that our guest speaker at the next meeting was to be Max Fatchen. In honour of the occasion, there was to be a limerick competition: the subject – Max Fatchen! Well, come the meeting, Max himself had forestalled us with a poem of his own. He spoke in his inimitable style – and I won the limerick competition! Not so surprising after all, when you know that one of my little quirks was that at the Annual Dinners of High School Heads, from the early 1960s onwards, I had the task of lightening up proceedings by singing a comic song, which I would have to compose in some spare hours during the preceding conference. It became sort of a tradition that I had licence to say rude things about departmental heads.

Within, deep down, the heart of my life goes on pumping the red stream of involvement with Bertha, our family and our friends. Overall though, my daily times with Bertha are the most rewarding moments of my present life. She's beginning to respond in ways that were perhaps unexpected a year ago. One little example happened at dinnertime, about a week ago. There was a lot of conversation in the room all around, and she looked at me inquiringly (well, she can't see, but I still say she 'looked at me'), and I said, 'I didn't say anything,' and she replied, 'Why not?' I said, 'Well, mainly because I didn't have much to say,' and she replied, 'Well, you could have said what a lovely wife you've got!' That's rewarding: it shows a reawakening.

And the progress continues. Recently, she has begun to volunteer comments, only to be stuck for an elusive word halfway through. But at Easter it all came together. I had been reading the Resurrection story, and at the words 'blessed are they that have not seen, and yet have believed', she said slowly in a reflective tone, 'It occurs to me,' a pause, then, 'It occurs to me that the other people who saw Jesus must have believed!'

Well, like Ulysses I am 'match'd with an aged wife'. But unlike Ulysses, I can have the best of both worlds: the company of my family here, at home: and the ability to follow the gleam of the untravelled world of the mind in company with my friends.

From the 1985 April luncheon, OHMS of SAHS (Old Head Masters of South Australian High Schools)

An Ode to OHMs

Old principals will meet sometimes
And so their minds are cast,
In prose and most uncertain rhymes
About their teaching past.

The schools in country realms remote,
A hundred in the shade;
The kids who tried to rock the boat,
The battle, grade by grade.

The end of term, the school reports,
The playground's shrilling clamour;
The drama of the annual sports,
The staff room's tea-stained glamour.

The Education's stern Gazette,
The gimlet-eyed inspectors;
The destinations wished upon
Those god-like men, Directors.

These faithful teachers had deep despairs
In duties so demanding.
They blessed the parents in their prayers
And asked for understanding.

Saint Peter at his gate is gruff;
He knows of Man's disasters;
'Pass on, for you've had hell enough,'
He says ... to old Headmasters

Max Fatchen, 2 April 1985

The winning laureate verse to mark the occasion of Max's visit:

O Fatchen, Max Fatchen,
Just what are you hatchin'
For pedagogues ageing and grey?
We give you fair warnin'
If we look to be yawnin' –
We're relaxin' with Fatchen. OK?

O Fatchen, Max Fatchen,
Your rhymin' is catchin' en.
I've been spouting such drivel all day,
The scouts from the 'Tiser –
(Would I tell you a lie Sir?)
Have hired me at twice Fatchen's pay.

Donald Stuart McDonald, 1985

GROWING OLD DISGRACEFULLY

Kym Bonython

Holding both the Distinguished Flying Cross and the Air Force Cross, Kym Bonython is a Companion in the Order of Australia, and a Knight in the Order of St John. After the war, Kym ran a Jersey cattle stud. Not only has he conducted a nationally broadcast jazz program for the ABC (1937–1976), but he has also arranged national concert tours by such artists as Duke Ellington, Count Basie, and Dave Brubeck. For 22 years Kym ran the Bonython Galleries in Adelaide and Sydney, and has produced several books on modern Australian art. For many years, Kym was a competitor and promoter of Rowley Park Speedway, Adelaide, and for two years he was Australian Hydroplane Champion. As chairman of the Jubilee 150 board, Kym presided over South Australia's sesquicentenary in 1986, and now is the convenor of the SA Council of Australians for Constitutional Monarchy. He was an elected delegate to the Australian Constitutional Convention, Canberra, 1998. It is 20 years since Kym's autobiography, *Ladies Legs and Lemonade*, was published.

An Australian flag fluttered in the garden of Kym's North Adelaide home, and we passed through a house decorated with scuptures on the way to his den where we sat amongst paintings, model bikes, shelves of CDs and hundreds of LPs.

A great pleasure in my life now, is to ride through the hills in autumn on the motorbike. To those who tell me, 'You're too old to be riding a bike,' I say, 'No, only too old to fall off it!' Like the motto of the Ulysses motorbike club, of which I'm a member, I aim to grow old disgracefully.

I rode my motorbike in Victoria Square a few years ago, parking the bike outside the place I was going. When I came out, there was an old fellow admiring the bike. He looked at me and he asked, 'How old are you, mate?' I replied, 'Seventy-five.' Thinking for a while, he said, 'You'll see eighty,' and then he walked off.

My grandfather, Langdon Bonython, who at one stage owned the *Advertiser*, rather rashly made a promise that if I came top of my class at St Peter's, he would give me what I wanted. Now, judging on past results, that was a fairly safe promise to make, but surprisingly I did come top that year. So, I went over to Carclew where my grandfather lived expecting to get what I wanted, to become somewhat crestfallen when given a stainless steel Big Ben pocket watch, suspended not on a gold chain, but on a black bootlace. I gratefully accepted the watch, but I put the hard word on my father to give me what I really wanted, a motorbike.

That's how, at the age of just over fifteen, I obtained a small Triumph motorcycle, and I've never been without a motorbike since. Even during the war, wherever we went, the units always had motorbikes. There was one shameful occasion when up at Darwin I rode the unit's motorcycle down the runway, standing on the seat, sort of balancing, turning, leaning this way and that. Then when the war ended I bought an army disposal motorbike followed by a couple of the classic motorbikes of that time, including an HRD Vincent, which was the Rolls Royce of motorbikes in those days.

Later, in 1966, when I wanted to get something a bit more exotic than the Honda I had at the time, I was persuaded to get a MV Agusta, ordered direct from the factory. I've had it for thirty-two years. It's purely and simply a touring bike. They had a racing version ridden by a fellow called Agostini, who for many years was the undisputed world champion, and who is actually coming out here for Phillip Island Race Day. He is going to do a sort of parade lap of the Grand Prix track accompanied by an array of MV Agustas.

Mine, I think, is the only one of the particular model in Australia and I've been approached to participate. If it was at Albert Park I'd say yes, but seeing that Phillip Island is quite a way, I may not participate. The prospect of perhaps living in a tent for three days no longer holds great appeal for me. I may, but I haven't decided.

I was never agile enough to be a bike racer. The successful bike riders were like jockeys, you know, small and agile. The champions were masters of balance and sort of all over the bike in their control. I'm notoriously clumsy. I still like watching that sort of racing, although it has lost a lot of the popularity it had. Sponsorship has got a lot to answer for because it's eliminated the former backbone of speedway, namely the back street mechanic. Unless you have a well-endowed sponsor, you're not in the event these days. One doesn't mind going racing and coming last, as long as you can win occasionally, but nowadays, unless you've got a sponsor, you're not even going to win occasionally. So that has altered the whole scene, probably not only in speedway, but in other sports also.

As a child in the 1920s, I used to be a regular speedway fan when it was started at Wayville, and I've been a follower ever since. From Wayville it moved to Camden, and then after the

War from Camden to Kilburn. Later it moved to Rowley Park, at Brompton, where I actually started driving a speed car in about 1951 or 1952. When the opportunity arose soon after to take over the Rowley Park lease, I did so, and I ran it for twenty years, not only as promoter, but also as a regular competitor.

You know, I used to live in Wakefield Street, and as a child I used to push down the footpath a model of the car my hero, Sir Henry Segrave, drove to gain the world land speed record. When I was at kindergarten, the teacher asked us to name the three greatest men that the world had ever known. My preferences in order of my interests were: Sir Henry Segrave; Jesus Christ; and Doctor Gunston, who lived next-door. But I never dreamt that sixty years later I'd be involved in bringing the real thing, the Formula One Grand Prix, right past what was then our front gate.

I did a program on ABC FM just before Christmas, and a couple of days later an old girlfriend rang me up and said, 'Do you remember when we were both seventeen and you drove me in your Amilcar around East Terrace? You said to me, "This would be a great place for a car race."' I replied, 'No, I'd forgotten that entirely,' although I suppose it remained in my thoughts.

I was always interested in car racing, but it was in 1980, when asked to chair the Jubilee 150 Board for planning the events to mark our state's 150th birthday (in 1986), that plans commenced for the Grand Prix to come to Adelaide. We had to come up with some major events to draw international attention to the state.

I was then on the City Council and I said to the town clerk, 'Is there any reason why we couldn't have a car race through the streets of Adelaide?' He said, 'No, not at all. The only thing that I'd suggest is that you try and pick a track that inconveniences the least number of residents as possible.' So that's basically how that track eventuated, although I never dreamt that we'd be allowed into Victoria Park.

Although I don't go regularly, I still follow car racing. But the sort of vehicles that I used to race in, which were little speed cars, are out of favour now, and I don't enjoy the races as much. When I left Adelaide to go to live in Sydney in 1973, I sold my interest in Rowley Park, and I stopped competing.

My Adelaide art gallery was established in 1960, but by the mid-60s I'd become aware that if I wanted to remain viable in that field, I had to expand my activities beyond Adelaide. In Sydney the top artists were beginning to be represented exclusively by a particular dealer, which meant the dealer gave them a living wage. I realised that if I stayed in Adelaide I'd finish up with just the people who weren't wanted by the top commercial galleries, so I expanded to Sydney.

I started off in Sydney in a very small gallery above a restaurant, with small rooms completely unsuitable for the scale of painting many of the artists were creating, like Brett Whiteley. So I built a big gallery around the perimeters of an enclosed courtyard. It was between two Paddington Streets on the site of a former sulphuric acid factory. The gallery was built around the perimeter and had this beautiful paved courtyard with willow trees and fountains in the middle. We actually moved up there and built an apartment above two wings of the gallery, staying there until the end of 1976, when we returned to Adelaide.

I went to a friend's funeral in Sydney a couple of years ago, and the person giving the eulogy said that the deceased had said to him shortly before his death that in 1954 Kym Bonython had infected him with an incurable disease – art collecting. He did quite well out of it because he befriended, as I did, many of the artists, and he had a very fine collection of paintings. I'm afraid it is a disease. My wife, not infrequently, asks, 'Are you trying to turn this house into a bloody art gallery?'

When I had an art gallery there was one definite rule. I recognised that a dealer should never pick the eyes out of a show until the public had had their opportunity to do so. When my house up in the hills, 'Eurilla', was burnt down in the Ash Wednesday bushfires, most of my collection was, of course, destroyed in the fire. This collection was either art that didn't sell during exhibitions, or else occasionally I'd go to a new artist's studio and be so taken with their work I'd buy something. Then they'd go on to become famous, or at least, a number of them!

I do gain a great satisfaction from art. Well, I grew up surrounded by it. My mother was quite perceptive for her generation, and she saw a lot in contemporary art that her contemporaries hadn't seen. I believe that if you expose people to something, they'll subconsciously start to appreciate it. I mean, whenever I had galleries, I always had suitable music of my taste playing in the gallery. Through exposure to that, people would be attracted to it.

My mother was very much admired and she was involved in all sorts of organisations like the Kindergarten Union and Mothers and Babies. Just before my fiftieth birthday she suffered her first stroke, so she didn't come to the party. Like her mother before her, the poor thing lingered on for years paralysed – we come from a fairly long-lived family on both sides. A gypsy once told me that I was going to live until I was ninety-three. Another gypsy told me I was going to be killed in an aeroplane crash in March. I don't really believe it, but I'm always quite glad when April comes and I've survived another March!

In 1994 I was opening an art show, and I said at the time that, 'If I had known fifty-two years ago, when I was lying petrified at the bottom of a split trench while Japanese bombs were raining all around, that I would be opening an art show in Adelaide tonight, I could have lived life a bit more recklessly!' The future didn't seem terribly promising then.

There were a lot of my friends who, alas, didn't survive the war and I feel that we've got a responsibility to them to try to preserve peace for future generations. I'm not a demonstrator or anything like that, but I just feel that those of us who survived have a responsibility to try and prevent that sort of thing happening again.

I was recently walking in King William Street and had somebody thrust a brochure into my hand about East Timor. I said, 'Are you really sure you want to talk to me seeing that I've dropped bombs on East Timor?' You know, flying in the Air Force, you didn't see the whites of the enemy's eyes, and I don't really want to know what damage those bombs did. I don't want to say that, 'On the fourth of February 1942, I was the one who dropped those bombs on the ships in Dili Harbour.' I don't really want to find out if they also killed twenty East Timorese in the process.

I know that our cause was justified, but being in the Air Force, one wasn't as conscious of death, other than the fact that sometimes your mates that were there in the morning were not there that night. There was one occasion when some of my squadron mates crashed, and I had to land over the burning wreckage of the plane. After I landed, I went to the wreck and my friends were all charred bodies and twisted limbs. Never again. If there was a crash, I never went in. So, I didn't sort of come face to face with death in the way that foot soldiers did.

Years later when I once visited Lombok, the only other

tourists there was a party of eighteen Japanese, and I soon found out from one who spoke English that they had been there during the war. They had come back to visit the graves of their fallen comrades. When I said, 'While you were here, I was flying around,' well! The cameras came out and the arms went around the shoulders and a pint of beer was thrust in my hands. I'm a lifetime teetotaller, you see, but the one time in my life that I've drunk a pint of beer was then, because I knew there was no way I could say, 'I'm sorry, I don't drink.' So I forced a pint of beer down for the sake of international harmony.

There were three different types of planes that I flew in action during World War II. First was the Lockheed Hudson, when I was in the Netherlands East Indies and Darwin. Then I came back and did a conversion course on an Australian-built Beaufort, which was a torpedo bomber, and I went immediately to Milne Bay. We were operating out of there until I came back again and was an instructor on those sort of planes for eighteen months. The final plane was the Mosquito, which was a photographic reconnaissance plane.

When flying the 'Skeeto', we used to take high-level photographs of Japanese airstrips north of Australia, but occasionally we would be required to do very low-level flights. I remember flying along the beaches of Bali and seeing bare-breasted girls waving as we went overhead. I never thought that I'd go back there much later and listen to jazz groups playing in five-star hotels!

My jazz interest started when my older half-brother, John (who later started SANTOS), went to Cambridge and came back with jazz records, the first that I had heard. Also, through a friend who lived around the corner from us, I heard my first Duke Ellington single. That was when I was about twelve, and I became an avid jazz fancier from then on.

When I was still at school, I used to send off to a place in New York called the Commodore Music Shop, which was not only a jazz music specialist shop, but also recorded jazz. Months later the records would arrive, and with fingers shaking in anticipation, I'd open the boxes, never dreaming that twenty or thirty years later I'd be bringing those very musicians to tour Australia.

So, you know, after that rare occurrence of coming top in 1935, my scholastic effort paled beside my interest in jazz, and I suppose, in the opposite sex. Jazz has pretty much played a large part in my life. During the war, wherever I went, even in the jungles of Netherlands East Indies, I always had my trusty wind-up gramophone and records. Of course, there was also my thirty-nine years of presenting a jazz radio program for the ABC on Friday nights at 9.30 pm. I remember that they always used to say, 'This is 1300 hours Greenwich Mean Time,' and then the program would commence.

Some years ago, I went to Canberra to be awarded something or other. I'd never met Sir Ninian and Lady Stephen, the Governor-General and his wife, and when I was finally introduced to Lady Stephen, her opening remark was, 'Oh, my husband and I used to lie in bed every Friday night and listen to your jazz program,' and I said to her, 'Well, that's hardly what I expected to hear from you.'

Dave Brubeck, whom I admire very much, said to me when I last spoke with him: 'Jazz is about going out on stage and taking chances. If you want to hear perfect music, listen to the classics.' Now, what he meant was that jazz is improvisation, and sometimes it works, sometimes it doesn't. There is that element of uncertainty. If you go out and improvise, and it 'comes off', it's magnificent. If not, it's abysmal. Another thing he said is, 'There is no such thing as a wrong note, so long as you can resolve it.' It is those sorts of things that are the backbone of why I find jazz so fascinating. There is that element of unpredictability.

My first school report, which also survived the fire, was rather perceptive. The headmistress said, 'Kym doesn't join with other children in set games, but prefers to swing on his own.'

I'm not a party or a club type. I'd much rather sit at home than go to parties and things. I'm a bit antisocial in a way, preferring to listen to music or read a book at home. There is an accumulation of books to read. The fact is I'm able to do a lot of things that are dear to my heart. I'm an avid movie-goer; I probably go three, or even four times a week. My movie taste is fairly broad, but sometimes absolutely an anathema to some. I mean, I was a great admirer of *Bad Boy Bubby*, but I took my doctor and his girlfriend, and they got up halfway through and said, 'If you like this, you're sick,' and walked out!

In the afternoon, I go into my study and sit down and watch what I've video-recorded the night before. My wife tells me that almost invariably I doze off. I know my father used to have a nap in his office every afternoon. Maybe the time's coming when I'll have to admit that I'm better off doing so.

Well, I'm the epitome of Bob Hawke's 'silly old bugger', which he used to describe a pensioner, because I'm always falling off ladders that I shouldn't be climbing. A year ago I fell of a retaining wall whilst pruning a rose that was getting out of control. I fell into the swimming pool and landed on my heel. I've always been a bit clumsy and even after that accident, I was just coming up the front steps here and I suddenly saw a rose that needed dead-heading, so I changed direction, fell over, and set myself back. I'm also conscious of the fact that as you get older things don't get better as quickly as they used to.

Of course, as you get older, you haven't got children around to do your bidding, so you're doing a lot of things yourself, which you logically shouldn't be doing. So I think that one sign of age is ignoring the logic of not doing things you shouldn't be doing. I'm only otherwise aware of ageing in that my memory for names and things is not what it used to be.

It's nice to see your family grow up. I've just become a great-grandfather for the first time. I have a lot of contact with my family. There are plenty of acquaintances, but I've only got a few really good friends that I see on a regular basis. My wife is much friendlier. She mixes better than I do, I'm afraid, but I like to think that I'm loyal to those friends I do have. Well, I've been told I am.

I just want to keep an active interest in things indicative of my priorities. Every now and again I have to get rid of another row of books to make room for another row of CDs. I have had to begin again my collection of music since the bushfire, because all the records I had were burnt in the fire. I've managed over the years to replace more than I ever thought I would, but still a number of my favourite records have not been re-issued, and all the personally signed albums by Duke Ellington and others, they're all gone.

There were so many things lost. You can replace the records, but not the films and the photographs; they're the irreplaceable things. We used to film every speedway meeting, and I took underwater movies in a two-man submarine in the 1950s and 1960s. I suspect I might have been the first person who got in amongst the seals at Seal Bay on Kangaroo Island when it was still a real business to get there because the road was particularly rough. There was film of the seals and it was just such a wonderful experience because they were all pushing and jostling, trying to look into the lens of the camera.

All those things went. All the pictures. I started making movies when I was twelve, and I had family films and things that were all burnt. The only film that I have is one I filmed illegally during the war of the two squadrons with which I was flying. Only a matter of weeks before the fire, the War Memorial in Canberra had heard about these films and borrowed them for copying. They sent the originals back just in time to be burnt, but I was able to get a copy of their copy.

People sometimes wonder how I coped with the bushfire. I usually say, 'I was so frantically busy with a dozen other things that it was just another problem.' I didn't have time to sit around and mope about it because I was too busy. If I hadn't had anything to keep me occupied, I might have. The fact is though that nine months later I had my first heart attack, but well, I attribute that more to the sort of things that I was eating, rather than worrying about the fire.

I've had a bit of heart trouble. My by-pass was done in May 1990 and I started going to the gym in August 1990. My only concession to healthy living is that I do go to the gym three times a week. I've religiously gone ever since then, sort of taking the attitude that if I say, 'Oh, I'm too tired to go today,' or, 'I can't be bothered,' that's the thin end of the wedge. So I force myself to go. I don't go into aerobic classes now, but I've got about fourteen or so routines that I do, and it takes me about forty minutes each time.

I'm deplorably dismissive of any dietary instructions my doctors have given me. I keep saying, 'I'd rather die with a smile on my face than be miserable on a Pritikin Diet.' I'm likely to stop off on the way home from the gym and get a cream puff or a meat pie. I've had my exercise, so I have a clear conscience! Going to the gym is a bit of a chore, but I sort of say, 'Well, if I do this, I can continue eating all those things I shouldn't be!' I mean, my biggest fear in life is to be told I've got diabetes and I've got to give up all those Fruchocs in the jar on my desk. It would be a fate worse than death.

Last time I was in New York, I went to dinner with Dave Brubeck. He was born in the same year that I was, and he had a heart condition develop about the same time as I did. When I went to this restaurant with him, and my food arrived, he looked at it with horror and said, 'You can't possibly be going to eat that!' It was french fries and things like that.

About three years ago now I had a heart attack after leaving the gym and I was in hospital for a week. When I came home a reporter from the *Advertiser* came to the house. I was quoted as saying, 'I hope I live long enough to eat a few more Vili's pies!' The next day, the sales manager of Vili's arrived on the doorstep with a great tray of them. So I said, 'Well, you can be assured that they'll be eaten at the wake!'

I am a strong advocate for the fact that one should, where possible, not subject oneself to living by text books. I agree with the simple philosophy that the moment you stop doing the things that bring you pleasure, then you might as well shut shop and wait till you die.

I've always striven to do what I can to the best of my ability. There was a pianist called Jaki Byard who I brought out on the most fantastic concert tour I ever arranged – Jaki was murdered at age seventy-six in New York in March 1999. But that was always my aim in life, to put on a good show that would be hard to better. Like improvisation, it didn't always happen, but I always strove to put on a good show.

Anyway, my doctor told me at one stage that it was alright to go to jazz concerts, but not to organise them. What I've done is I've given up arranging national tours. Occasionally, if there is somebody in Australia that I particularly like, I might organise an Adelaide concert, but I've given up trying to arrange concerts in Melbourne, Sydney, Brisbane, and so on. It's too much of a hassle, although most jazz people are lovely and easy to get on with, unlike so many of their 'rock' contemporaries.

I don't travel much these days. When I was running the Speedway and doing concert promotions, I had a justification for going overseas to select competitors for our summer, which was their winter, and to suss out the rising talent in the concert field. But now that I haven't got those sort of activities, I don't travel much.

The last time I was in England, I went to Cornwall and actually sat at the big table in the house of my ancestor after whom I was named, Reskymer Bonython, Sheriff of Cornwall, who was born in 1592. To sit there was quite a thrill. I'm grateful to my relations who have gone to the trouble of researching the family tree and knowing about our origins. I mean, they can trace my family back to the 1200s, in an unbroken line.

I was sent a cutting from a newspaper reporting that the old family property in England, which still bears the name of 'Bonython', was about to be purchased by Rowan Atkinson. One of the features of the property that I noticed when I was there were fourteen of those giant propellers for wind-generated power. The English paper surmised that Rowan Atkinson would have endless fun racing around his property flapping his arms generating power. However, the sale fell through due to a disagreement regarding the commercial mineral water rights on the estate.

My grandfather instilled, in all his grandchildren, a respect for our ancestors. I think my grandfather has been an inspiration to all of us because he was a very public-spirited, generous person, who expected a lot from his family. I'm sure our careers have been inspired by his example. He was also a religious person, a particularly strong and regular church-goer, which I can't claim to be.

I believe in God but I was probably more involved with religion as a student at St Peter's College than now. I am a member of the Order of St John of Jerusalem that has a religious basis, as the order of service dates back to the Middle Ages. I do envy people who find satisfaction and consolation in a strong religious belief. I admire them and sometimes wish I had the same spiritual beliefs that they had. I've already discussed my funeral with Archbishop Ian George to ensure that the music that will be played on that occasion (which is already on tape on my front hall table) will not be offensive to the church.

I try not to think badly of anyone. I'm sort of reluctant to be uncharitable toward others. I try to give people the benefit of the doubt and attribute motives that are not as bad as their behaviour might imply. But I've never claimed to be an intellectual. I think Max Harris used to think I was a bit of a philistine, but as I say, I'm more interested in going my own way and hoping that in the process I won't step on other people.

After mid-1987, when my involvement with the Jubilee 150 ended, I was virtually unemployed until 1993, when I was approached by the Australians for Constitutional Monarchy (ACM) to start a branch in South Australia. Like a lot of these committees, it inevitably comes down to one or two people being expected to do everything. I think that's going to have to change in the next few months, seeing as I turn eighty next year. I've already said that I really don't feel I can do everything I have been doing over the past years. It is time-consuming and occasionally exhausting.

The basis for my commitment to the ACM is that there are a number of high-profile urgers for a republic who are pushing it when the general public is basically apathetic about it. There are polls requesting people to list the things that politicians should be spending their time on, and the word 'republic' rarely, if ever, appears.

I mean if, in years to come, the monarchy doesn't exist anymore in England, well obviously we'll have to have a look at it again. The fact of the matter is that there's been no interference from England for many years. The ties have legally been severed for the past thirty or forty years. So we're talking of spending what would amount to maybe a billion dollars to give us something that we've already got.

I think that there's no reason why we should be ashamed of the good things that we got from England that have made us into one of the most stable countries in the world to which people from troubled republics are anxious to immigrate. I was a little upset, as an elected member of the Constitutional Convention, when some of the young republican representatives, immigrants from elsewhere, were urging that we become a republic when Australia must have appealed to them as a good place with a good future. Now, that being so, why would they be so keen to change it into a situation that eventually could give rise to the very conditions from which they were so keen to get away?

It is a red herring about the Head of State not being Australian. The Queen is only a *symbolic* Head of State, as the *real* Head of State, the constitutional Head of State, is the Governor-General, who has long been an Australian. I think that to replace the Governor-General with a president will mean further politicisation and centralisation of even more power in Canberra than there is at present.

I don't know if I would have felt as passionate about this when I was younger. Unlike Max Harris, with whom I went to school, I was never a motivated force for some ideal, but I suppose, having served for five and a half years during World War II, and with the passing of the years, I do have an admiration for the Queen. Also, I disagree violently with people who say, 'Oh, we can't have Charles as our King!' If you'd had photographers up pine trees with telephoto lens in the time of Henry VIII, well! It's not the behaviour of the individual that is the issue, rather it's the system that has proved itself over hundreds of years.

I guess today, in many areas, I'm a bit of the conservative. I don't like much of the art favoured by present-day experts, and I find quite a lot of jazz that is performed by people like Winton Mersallis has a ton of technique, but not very much soul. Rossini said: 'What is old is not always good. What is new is not always better.' I think that that can apply to art, literature, music and even government.

So, these days, in addition to my commitments to ACM, and to a few other organisations with which I'm involved, I indulge myself by going to the movies, listening to music, and riding the bike. Most days I'm out on the bike, even if only just to go into town.

I just think, so long as you don't hurt others, do what gives you pleasure. Also, don't sort of throw in the towel and just sit around the house with a rug over the knees and wait for the end. Really, if I weren't doing the things that I'm doing, that I like doing, I'd probably collapse in a heap. In the words of one of my favourite wordsmiths, the late film-maker Samuel Goldwyn, 'If I could drop dead at this moment, I'd be the happiest man alive!'

BUONA, BELLISSIMA

Vincenzo Perrini

In 1956, not only did a friend of Vincenzo Perrini 'call him out' to Australia from Naples, but the same friend ensured that Vincenzo had a job to start at the Holden factory the day after his arrival in Adelaide. Vincenzo immigrated to Australia on the ship *Fairstar*. Previously, he had 'worked the land' in Italy. It was several years before Vincenzo was able to bring his wife and sons to Australia. Following their reunion, Vincenzo lived with his family at Kilkenny, Woodville, and later at Seaview Downs. For twenty-five years, although never being a driver of a motor vehicle, he worked on the press at the factory producing bumper bars for Holden cars. Vincenzo, a healthy eighty-eight year old who never consults a doctor, enjoys a busy life tending his home garden, processing its produce, and helping his family with their various business pursuits.

We needed an interpreter to translate Vincenzo's Napolitano Italian dialect for us. His answers to our questions invariably resulted in gales of laughter from his wife and daughter-in-law sitting around the kitchen table with us.

All day I work very hard! I've got the backyard. I've got chickens. I've got rabbits. I plant things – tomato, beans. So I work in the garden and I look after the chooks and the rabbits. The chooks are good layers of eggs – about seven or eight a day. Sometimes the chooks end up in the cooking pot – in the oven, or on the stove. The rabbits end up in the cooking pot too. I take the head off first! Well, I take the skin off too, put it into the rubbish, and the council takes it away.

There are vegetables all year round. I grow things like fennel, salad greens, tomatoes, cauliflower, broccoli, cucumber, and watermelon. For manure I use blood and bone, and it grows good. The tomatoes grow very well.

With the tomatoes, I make about five or six hundred bottles of tomato sauce for myself, my family, my relatives, and my friends. I don't do that on the one day! I make it about three, four different times. And the tomato sauce is 'buona, bellissima'! Very, very, very good. The best! I've got it all in my head – all the process of making the tomato sauce, making it in the bottle, everything.

For the sauce, I've got my own tomatoes, and then I have to buy them as well. I haven't got enough land here to grow that many tomatoes. But the first thing about good tomato sauce is to get the good tomato, the one they call 'roma' tomatoes. That's the first thing. With other tomatoes, the sauce comes good, but not as good as roma tomatoes. Roma – he makes a nice, you know, solid sauce, and very red, you know. That's important.

This is not a sauce for putting on pies and pasties! This is good Italian tomato sauce. The best for pasta – to use with spaghetti, macaroni and all other kinds of pasta. Whether I make enough to last all year for everyone depends. It depends how the family and the friends eat! Sometimes it is enough. Sometimes it isn't, you know.

Now, I have been doing the almonds. There is a tree in the backyard. I get the almonds, I let them dry in the sun, then with a bottle I crush the shell, and after I clean them, I boil them in water, take the skin off, and then I eat them! If you want to keep them, you then have to roast them in the oven. They can keep quite a long time if you store them in jars. They keep as long as you like. This is not just for us. This is for the family. Whenever they come and visit, we put them on the table and they eat them.

By 5.30 each morning, I'm up. Every morning, at 6.30, I watch SBS on the TV because they have the news direct from Italy. So I start in the garden around seven. I finish around eleven. Then I come inside, I eat, I have a glass of wine, and since about the last fifteen years, I go then to have a nap for an hour, or an hour and a half. After that I don't work anymore with my backyard. I might just sit outside, alfresco, or I might go and see my sons, to help my sons.

My son Tonino has set up a winery, Perrini Estate Winery, at Meadows. I might go there and I help him, you know, bottling wine, drinking wine! But I do whatever there is to do. If there is something I see that has to be done, I'll do it. I helped them at the winery when it was establishing. Mostly when they established the vineyard. Well, we planted about sixteen thousand plants, and I helped sometimes with that. But, for sure I help drink the wine!

When I was younger, and the kids were still little, I used to make wine. It was me who taught my son how to make wine. As you well know, 'the lamb has to learn from the ram', as they say in Italian. I'm the ram, and the kids have to learn from me.

My favourite wine is sauvignon blanc! Well, not really. I drink red wine. It is good for older men to drink wine. Very healthy. You never die from wine! You should drink one litre a day! Maybe not, but only when you eat, with meals, two glasses. If you don't eat, no wine. But two glasses per meal, that's about the limit.

And I have another son who is a hairdresser at the St Agnes Shopping Centre. It's for men and for women, and he's got three or four people working for him. Sometimes I go and help him myself. If there's nothing to do, I just sweep all the hair on the floor. I don't do the hair-style! But, sometimes, when I haven't got anything to do, I just go there.

At this stage, for my sons, the responsibility is theirs, but I can help them, you know.

A grandson had a supermarket down the road. It was a business on Brighton Road. He has sold it now, but I did quite a lot of work there too. I used to go there once a day on foot. Down the hill and up the hill. I still walk there, and I come back. It is very good for you and your legs. You have to move. You have to keep moving. If you start sitting down, you can't walk anymore, as it's no good for you. You have to move your body.

Youth is youth, and old age is a bit of a bastard! Well you become a bit like, restricted, when you are older. You know, you can't hurry to do the things you want to do. Also, when I was young, I was strong. If there was a fight or some threat, I could do something, but these days I can't. When you get older, you can't defend yourself anymore.

But certainly there are many good things when you are older. You can do things you like because you've got the time. You don't have to rush, and you can do it at your own pace. You can stop when you want to. As a young man, you had to work and everything. Now, in old age, you can do things when you want to. So, you've got more freedom.

When you are older, you should eat well, sleep well, keep happy, and don't get too worried. It is good not to think too much. Not about the past, either. I don't do that. If you're doing that, that's why you go a bit soft in the head! Just leave it. It's not a good thing. I just thank God that He's given me the health, and that my life is like this.

I like eating everything. Spaghetti, macaroni, meat, pasta – everything. I'm always eating! The 'boss' does the cooking. That is, my wife! We have been married for fifty-two years. That's a long time, right?

Our family gets together every Sunday. This is at dinner-time, because they have to close the business. We may get together here or at their place, it just depends. Sometimes somebody can't make it because of a work commitment kind of thing, but normally we are together every Sunday. From the two sons, we have four grandchildren. They are all married except one, and there is a great-grandchild. To be a good Italian grandfather, if you've got some money, you give it to them! Well, maybe not really!

I enjoy these days being visited by a friend, or visiting friends and playing cards, which I like. We play a game called Tresette, meaning three sevens, which is played with Italian cards, Napolitan cards, that are smaller cards. The other games are Scopa and Briscola. The type of Italian that we speak is Napolitano – Napolitan. There are a lot of people in Adelaide who speak that. All of Naples is here!

I arrived here in Adelaide on the 14 February 1956, and on the fifteenth I was working. I had a friend who could read a newspaper, and he got the job out of the newspaper. So, they took me to the Holden Factory, and there they say, 'Oh, yeah,' and I started. The friend who did this was the one who 'called me out'. To come to Australia, you had to have someone to 'call you'. I had these people make this request for me to come here, and that's the reason why I came here to Adelaide, and not Melbourne.

Here in Australia you can earn more money. Well, you know, in Italy you just work on the farm for very little, and here, you can make a nice life for yourself. It was a very good decision. And then later, after two years, I called my wife and the children. Anyway, I had to borrow two thousand dollars to bring my wife over, and I made this debt with a bank that used to lend money to migrants for that sort of thing.

I was very happy when I had the money to bring my family over here, and when eventually we got all together in a house. It was very hard without the family. At Holden's, it was very hard work too. We all liked to joke with each other, but mostly we were working. Luckily I managed with just speaking Italian because they were all Italians. There were no English! The leading hand, and the boss of that section, they were all Italian. I think there were sixteen thousand Italians! But my grandchildren speak everything. They speak Italian, English, French!

In 1960 I went back to Italy. I did a long trip to the United States, Canada, Italy and then back to Australia. I only went back once because later I didn't have anybody, any relatives, in Italy. One sister went to Canada, and the other one stayed in Italy, and they are dead now. So, that's the only time I went back. There is nothing really that I miss about Italy. Not really.

Sometimes we did go away to Sydney or Melbourne. We'd take a plane, or a bus. We did move around, and we'd have people coming over to see us. Friends, people who come from the same town. That still happens sometimes, that they visit us. There is nothing else really that I want to do. Not really. I've done everything, and I don't feel like being driven around much anymore. I like reading the newspaper, *il Globo*, that comes from Melbourne and Sydney. Sometimes I watch movies on SBS. And the only thing I would like is for the government to make it easier for older people in Australia by giving them more money for the pension!

I'm eighty-eight now. My mother died reasonably early, when she was fifty-five. My father lived to be an old man, as he was eighty-four years old, and very well, but then he had like a stroke, a paralysis. He'd always been very healthy. My father, and now myself, we don't know anything about hospital and doctors. I don't need one. I don't understand doctors! I have no tablets, and I've got a good stomach. I can eat and drink, so I'm very well. Perhaps I've been lucky, but I think I've lived well.

I'm not really thinking about being older. I feel young. I always feel young. And I don't really think about how old I might get to be. But, whatever God is going to give me, I'll take it!

RUST-FREE

Bill Schmitt

During World War II, Bill Schmitt served five years overseas with the 2/3 Machine Gun Battalion, Australian Imperial Forces, fighting in the Middle East and Java. Bill was captured by the Japanese Army and survived imprisonment at the infamous Changi Prison, Singapore. In 1994, Bill was made a Member of the Order of Australia for his contribution to ex-prisoners of war and the veteran community. For the past twenty-three years Bill has been Secretary of his Unit, and for nineteen years, State Secretary of the Ex-Prisoners of War Association of SA Inc. He followed 'Weary' Dunlop as Federal President of the Ex-Prisoners of War Association, and he is now the elected Patron-in-Chief, having followed the Governor-General in that role. Aged in his early eighties, Bill still relentlessly works voluntarily for the veteran community, and is actively involved with many Department of Veteran Affairs committees. Previously, Bill worked at management level for the pastoral company Elder Smith Co. Ltd, and in that role lived with his family at Tumby Bay, Kapunda, Keith, Cleve, and Cummins.

Bill came to us for his interview, at the Royal District Nursing Services of SA Business Centre. He bounded up the steep stairs those twenty years younger have trouble climbing and hurried off to a meeting after an interview filled with laughter, despite the serious topics we discussed.

This week I had a game of golf for the first time in six months. I used to play golf in my younger days with a handicap of five, but at the moment, I haven't time to play. I enjoy golf, but I enjoy what I'm doing, so you've got to make up your mind what you want to do.

I mean, when I came home from the war, and more so since I've retired, I've looked back on things. I think particularly of the prisoners of war – POWs, although I represent a lot of veterans other than POWs. Thirty-six per cent of POWs never came home. Eight thousand and thirty-four died in Japanese prisoner of war camps. The biggest death rate was in Borneo, at Sandakon, where there were only six survivors out of about seventeen hundred Australians.

I often say that I'd like to take the younger people, who weren't even born when the war was on, up to the war graves in Singapore, to look at the headstones. Don't worry about the names, but just look at the ages, you know, eighteen to twenty-five, twenty-six. There are *thousands* of them! Also, with the 8th Division that went to Singapore, and those of us in the Middle East, including those that were killed in the actual fighting, four in every ten didn't come back.

But 1995 alerted a lot of people to what the second world war was all about. That was the 'Australia Remembers' year. We went to schools to tell people about it, so it came to the forefront. Today, attendances at Anzac Day marches are far better, and that's the result of 1995, I think. What turned people against war was the Vietnam War. I mean, people got tired of it. They didn't want to talk war anymore, and I don't blame them.

The government's got a duty to the survivors – those men and women who put up with it. I've been fortunate, touch wood. I mean, I did go through a long period of sickness in and out of Daws Road Repatriation Hospital for about a year after I came home, but I recovered. A lot of them died. We had a lot of deaths the first five years after the war, and then there are those who have since died.

We had a dreadful job about five years ago trying to do something when a POW died, and you couldn't get his widow a war widow's pension. As national president, I had to be persistent. There were two or three different ministers during that period. At last they agreed for the widows of POWs to automatically become 'war widows'. So there was less work after that.

There was a big pat on the back, and I think as a result, I was given a Meritorious Service Award from the Federal Association, but that's not what matters. I just feel if there's anyone deserving of this, it's those widows. They had to put up with some cranky husbands, you know. They weren't all well, and the wives nursed them and stuck by them, rearing children under difficulties. That applies to a lot of ex-servicepeople, but more particularly to POWs, I think.

I mean the POWs were my own group. Somebody's got to fight for them.

There are other things that need to be done. A widow, not long ago, rang me at 6.20 in the morning to tell me that her husband had died in bed alongside her. She said, 'He always said to ring you if anything happened to him.' So I organise funerals and goodness knows what. You'd be surprised how many people haven't made any funeral arrangements. They don't like to talk about it. There are some who have pre-paid funerals. Anyway, the widows know that I can't keep in touch with them forever, but I keep in touch with them the first few months. I give a ring every now and then to see how they're going.

Today, the reason I still go on with all this is that although the Department of Veterans' Affairs (DVA) is very good, a lot of POWs don't know what benefits are available. So when I get a spare hour or two, I slip over to Daws Road and see who's in hospital and talk to them, finding out what pension rates they're on, *if* they are on a pension. You'd be surprised how many POWs are only on twenty or thirty per cent, some on *none*, and either don't realise their rights, or had fall-outs with the DVA in the early days, so they won't go back. All that sort of thing. The government is a lot more liberal, particularly towards POWs, but you've got to get the message out to the people as to what is available to them.

To give you some background – I was stationed in the country most of my working life, with Elder Smith's. I was born at a place called Cowell. My father was in charge of railway gangs re-laying the railway lines over on the West Coast, and there were five of us children in the family. I was the eldest, and although I'd done pretty well at school, I had to leave in 1932, as it was the middle of the Depression. Dad had taken a big cut in salary from the government at that time, so I found work with a Farmers Union Commission Agent and Grain Merchant.

Anyway, when I came home from the war, I had the opportunity to join Elders and eventually became a branch manager at various places in the country. The company was expanding, it being just after the war, and promotions were going on pretty well. Later I came to Adelaide to be in charge of finance with the firm, when I became too old to jump fences and stockyards in the country. Also, our son was coming back from America to do his PhD, so he needed accommodation in the city. I retired when I was sixty-one.

In the country, being a 'bird of passage', as they called us people who had to move from place to place, you needed to always become involved with local activities – Returned and Services League, golf clubs – and you were the secretary or president of something, you know. I'd made up my mind that I'd get away from that sort of thing when we moved to the city, but I didn't quite know what I was going to do – what I wanted to do.

I did become very closely associated with the 2/3 Machine Gun Battalion Association, which was my own unit. Well, they'd always had joint secretaries. A fellow called Charlie Shea was the secretary then, and he said to me one day, 'You're going to retire, so what about coming in and helping me with this?' His previous three co-secretaries had all died, so I said, 'On one condition, Charlie, and that is if anyone is going to die, it's got to be you and not me!' And that's what did happen! Poor old Charlie died a year or two later, and I've had the job ever since.

As a result of that position, I was 'sucked in', I suppose, to take over as the state secretary of the Ex-POWs Association. They couldn't get a secretary, so the president of the day came and pleaded with me to go and do it. I said I'd do it for six months, and I'm still doing it, nineteen years later. Through that role, I had five years as federal president of the Ex-POWs Association, taking over from 'Weary' Dunlop. In 1942 I was captured in Java with Weary, who was one of our doctors, so I knew him very well.

Anyhow, during my first two years as federal president, we started to put together a program to take people up to Singapore for a commemoration service to celebrate fifty years since the fall of Singapore. I was half-way through that when my two-year term finished, so the federal executive said, 'No, you've started it, so you finish it.' I continued as federal president, and went back to Singapore in 1992 with about a thousand people,

I suppose, from all over Australia. There were also wives, widows, and what have you. Later I was elected as patron-in-chief of the association, which is an honour.

Also, through being state secretary of the Ex-POWs Association, I've been dragged into lots of other things, you know, because the DVA has different committees, and you're the nominee to represent the POWs in this and that. For the DVA in general, I'm a member of the Joint Ventures Steering Committee that distributes funds to ex-service organisations for projects, and I'm also a member of the Commemoration Consultative Committee. I'm involved at Daw Park Repatriation Hospital, as a member of the South Australian Monitoring and Treatment Committee (overseeing the transfer of the hospital to the public health system), as a member of the Future Direction Consultative Group, and deputy chairmen of the hospital's museum.

I'm also currently chairman of the Consultative Council of Ex-Service Organisations for South Australia. This is a group of about thirty ex-service organisations, including; the Totally and Permanently Incapacitated Association (TPI), War Widows, Legacy, and all those other groups that look after the welfare of ex-service people. It is not in opposition to the RSL. In fact, the RSL is on the committee, but it is another means of bringing up the problems we've got to go to the government, and things like that.

Fortunately with this council, all the work that we had in the early days is over and done with, and we haven't got so many problems. I mean, there's always a few little niggly things, but it's easing now because there are a lot less veterans. Also, over the years, we've all gained a pretty good standing with government and with the DVA.

I think that's about all the committees.

I suppose I would average two to three meetings a week. I'm fairly fit with just one complaint that I've suffered for many years, called trigeminal neuralgia. It's a dreadful disease, but fortunately I'm in the care of an expert neurologist who goes to Daws Road, and there is a drug I can take. I start taking it the moment I get the first tinge. Otherwise the neuralgia will start with a sudden pain, and it will 'tic' for a couple of days, or it might go for a week. If you let it set in, it's terrible. The medication will hold it, but you have to take heavy doses, and you'll get around like a stunned rabbit for a day or two. At least it keeps it under control.

To be truthful though, when I was working, I was a very heavy smoker, and I think if I hadn't stopped when I did, I certainly would have been dead in five years. Before the war, I couldn't afford to smoke much, but I smoked a lot after I got home. Of course, during the POW days, we didn't have much access to cigarettes or tobacco, much as we craved it. I always said, 'If I ever get out of this place, I'll never give up smoking.' But anyway, later, while I was manager at Keith, I knew that there was no way known that I could carry on with the job if I kept smoking, so I gave it up on 19 January 1964. Remember it as only yesterday! I've never smoked since.

I was about nine-and-a-half stone then, and I put on about a stone and a bit, to be about two pounds under eleven stone, and I've stayed that weight. And I'm sure that if you can stay the same weight over the years when you get older, that's half your problem solved. I'm not a big eater. I suppose that may be a result of the starvation as a POW. I never eat enough to feel uncomfortable, and I don't eat a lot at midday. We always have a fairly substantial one-course meal at night, and probably some fruit, particularly at the time of the year when there's plenty of fruit about.

The other thing is that I think you can worry about yourself too much, can't you? I mean, you get a little pain here, and a little pain there, and you start popping pills, and that's the end of you, you know. I know that people get sick, and then you've got to take pills, but I resist them as much as I can.

Also, I don't dawdle. When I move, I move quickly, as quick as I can, but I'm getting slower with age. I mow my own lawns and garden and what have you. I've never laid down during the day either. Mind you, sometimes I feel a bit tired, but there's no future in that! Night-time is the time to sleep.

I have no trouble in remembering things that happened fifty years ago – a wonderful memory in that regard, but if you said to me, 'What did you do yesterday?', I'd have to stop and think for a moment. I think that's probably applicable to anyone my age, anyway.

I don't think that I'm ageing. If you start thinking about ageing, well that's when you age. That's my idea of it. When I was sixty, I don't think I even wondered, 'Will I be alive when I'm eighty?' But now I have a big ambition to see this year out and the year 2000 in.

There's always something on. We've a POW reunion in Melbourne coming up. My son in Perth turns fifty this year, so I guess we'll go over for that. And my daughter in Melbourne, her second daughter's making a debut, and we'll go to Melbourne for that. So, there's always something to look forward to.

We have three children. One daughter lives here in Adelaide. We have eight grandchildren, two here, three in Perth, and three in Melbourne, from twenty-four down to ten years old. They're great. If only we had them all closer to us, though. I remember them all well when they were little babies, one or two, three, four or five – innocent little things, you know. Great!

Our youngest grandson is in Melbourne. There's been a thing come out in the *Advertiser* this week, a little album, and you've got to collect the pictures of marine creatures to stick in the album. I think it's great, so I've been getting them all this week for him. I did the same a few months ago with animals. He has to peel them off and put them in the album. I love my grandkids, and I think they think I'm alright too, but we only really have close association with the two who are here, and that's day-to-day.

I knew of my wife, her family, and friends of hers before the war, but a relationship only developed when I came home that September. We married the following April. We have been married for fifty-three years in April, a good married life. I believe that it helps if you've got a good marital situation, with your wife on side with you. That helped me a great deal during my work with the stock company, where I'd be away long hours all day. But, if you have a good relationship, mutual agreement, and trust and faith in one another, I think that goes a long way to a happy outlook.

Only a few of the POWs didn't marry. For a lot of them though, marriages unfortunately didn't work out, and they married a couple of times, but most of my friends have been much like me with relationships that have gone on and on. In those days, your word was your bond, and that's it.

I just feel lucky to be here. A lot of POWs still hate and detest the Japanese, of course, and I can understand it, you know, living there and seeing what happened to us – the torture and things that they did. I've said many, many times that anyone who was a POW of the Japanese, whatever his thoughts of them are, that person should be *respected*, but I don't think we've got a right to go and sow the seeds of hate for future generations. Weary and I discussed it a lot, and personally,

I think it's pointless to go on hating people for the rest of your life. I mean, it doesn't achieve anything, and anyway the people who were involved and inflicted all the cruelty, they're probably all dead and gone.

I'm fully convinced that I'm dealing with a new generation of Japanese. I've met a lot of them. In fact, in 1992, when I was in my hotel room up in Singapore, the High Commissioner rang me one morning and said: 'We've got a Japanese film crew here that would like to interview you. Are you happy about doing it?' And I said, 'Yes, I'll talk to them.'

So, I met with this young Japanese journalist, about thirty-two, thirty-three, who had spent a few years in America and could speak fluent English. He had a crew with him – a girl and a couple of other chaps, and cameras and what have you. They came to my hotel room, and the first thing he said was: 'Look, I want you to tell me everything the Japanese did. I know nothing. I wasn't born. I've never been told, and there's nothing written in our history books in Japan about the war.' So I told him everything that I thought he should know. At the same time I thought there's nothing much taught in our schools either. My kids never learnt anything about the Japanese in the war and what happened, and probably a good thing they didn't.

I can't see any point in hating people. I mean, it's not my nature to hate people. I can't do it. It's meaningless and pointless passing it on to other people, like one of the atrocities that I saw when two Dutch people were beheaded. Those sorts of things are frightening. I just put it behind me, because if you didn't, you'd be a wreck.

After all, the Japanese treated their own people much the same. If we offended in our army, you would be sent up through the proper channels to be fined or something, but the

Japanese didn't have that sort of discipline. In Changi I was badly beaten up, knocked unconscious, out on the aerodrome. If one of their soldiers did something wrong, he was punished there and then too: slapped up, bashed, kicked, made to stand to attention out in the sun, or all sorts of things.

I came out of Changi still believing in God. The Japanese had a cruel way of issuing punishment, and they did torture some of our fellows to death, but it wasn't God's wish that they do it. Also, I think there is something hereafter.

Changi hasn't harmed me, you know. I mean, I know it's harmed other people, but I think it's your ability to put it behind you, to forget, that helps. When we came home, we were told: 'Get back to work. Forget about what's happened to you. Go back and get into it. The quicker you get back to work, the better.' And I think that's true.

I'm just so fortunate to be able to look ahead and to have been able to meet a lot of good people. I've enjoyed meeting people and cementing a *lot* of friendships. That's stood me in good stead and makes me happy.

Mostly, I think about my school days, younger days, and later life, after we came back. I remember my discharge. They'd given me some wheatgerm oil out at Daws Road because my eyesight had suffered. This doctor was examining us on North Terrace for discharge, and he said, 'Now, what do you have to complain about?' I said, 'Oh, nothing much, except my eyesight's not all that good.' Right alongside the window was another building, a brick building, and he said, 'What sort of wall is that out there?' I said, 'It's a brick wall.' He said, 'Oh well, there's nothing wrong with your eyes.' It was like that, just like that, but that's fifty-odd years ago, and now it's a different world.

I will always remember my poor old mother and father

meeting me out at Daws Road. When I came home I was forty-two kilograms or something, and I remember dear old Dad saying to me, 'God boy, what have they done to you?' But I often think to myself that even though we suffered, what about my mother? She had four of us in the services. I joined the army the same day as one of my brothers. Two other brothers joined the airforce.

Three of us were overseas when I was captured. Mum received, in May 1942, a letter to say that I was missing. Now, I used to regularly write home at least once a week, or once a fortnight, and she hadn't heard any word from me for some weeks. Mum got a letter through the post saying, 'Private WH Schmitt, SX9929, is missing.' So, they unfortunately didn't know whether I was dead or alive. In July she was sent another letter to say they still didn't know what had happened to me. So that's dreadful for a woman, for a mother. Then, in November, a letter was sent to her confirming that I was a prisoner of war in a camp in Java. Fortunately, all four of us did return.

I recently saw the film *Saving Private Ryan*. Just a typical American blood and guts film! I was in the Syrian Campaign, and I was there when two thousand of us met sixty thousand Japanese in Java. We had three days of combat, and lost a lot of men, but the battle scenes in the film were over-exaggerated. The story is quite good though, and I know of something similar. There was a farmer at Kapunda, an old client of Elders, and he had three sons. I think they were all in the airforce, and two of them were shot down and killed in action over Europe. Their third son was immediately brought back to Australia and discharged.

My favourite uncle fought in France during the first world war, and he won a Military Medal. I was named after him when I was born in 1918. Well, when I joined the army I took the train up to Pt Broughton and went to see him, as I knew nothing about the army – I was saluting the cook, or anyone in uniform! My uncle said, 'See if they will let you join the machine gunners.' He was a machine gunner, and he explained how you had the artillery as one line of fire, and then the machine gunner in between, and the infantry out front. So that's how I got into the machine gunners.

He aged very, very well, living until he was ninety-one or ninety-two. Didn't have a lot of sickness or illness. He was chairman of the District Council up there, and heavily involved in local affairs. Well respected.

People sometimes say that I don't look like I'm over eighty. I don't feel any different than I did when I was sixty, except I think I'm a bit slower. The good thing about being older is that, well, I think you're respected. People say, 'You're doing a good job.' My grandchildren seem to think I'm a bit of alright. They've got a certain amount of pride for what I've done, and what I'm doing, and for my service to the country, and things like that. You don't look for that. When I was given the AM, it was a big surprise to me. It came out of the blue. When I was made patron and things like that, you get a kick out of it, a buzz, but you don't set out in life to *get* these things. But if they come, you're very proud to get them, naturally, and your family are too.

My attitude has always been a determination to get things done. If opportunities came along I took them, even if it meant working day and night to make the best of it.

That attitude may have helped me a bit in Changi. I've said this many times. In Changi I had fourteen or so bouts of malaria, and I don't know how many bouts of dysentery and things like that. Fortunately, I never got cholera, but you would get so sick that sometimes you'd think, 'Oh God!' However, over the years you'd think, 'You've survived all this!' If they'd said to me in the first six weeks of being captured that I had another three and a half years to endure, well, that may have been the finish. 'To hell with this. I'm not going to put up with this for three and a half years.' But you always thought, 'Well, another month and I could be out!' So you'd fight your way through it. But I saw plenty of my mates die, and I'm sure that some lost the will to live.

It was a hopeless situation of course, when you're down and you're eating so little – four ounces of rice a day. Changi was a shocking place for food and you ate anything that was around. There wasn't a cat or a monkey or a dog to be seen in the place, you know! You eat anything if you're hungry.

It's a matter of looking positively at things. You don't have to think that because you're ageing, you're going to be limited in your activities. If you've got good health, or reasonably good health for your age, then there's no reason in the world that you just can't carry on and do the things that you like to do. But you've got to do things that you enjoy doing. I mean, there are tasks that you don't like, but if you enjoy doing whatever, well, continue to do it.

I enjoy what I'm doing now – making contact with people, mixing with people, helping them. That's the main thing, helping people without gain, only satisfaction. It may even cost a bit. I think I've worn out a car working for the Ex-POW Association, through just running around.

Last year, the Repatriation Commission was eighty years old, and here in South Australia the DVA invited Brian Hall, who is a great mate of mine, and me to their celebrations because we were both turning eighty at about that time too. We were both given a Certificate of Appreciation from the Minister of Veterans' Affairs for our service to the veteran community. I had earlier been given a Certificate of Recognition for my services when I was the chairman of the Commemoration Committee for 'Australia Remembers'. In South Australia, I was responsible for putting the program together, the march and the concert and all those sort of things.

Well, I hope that I can carry on with what I am doing for some time yet. At least another five years, because I think that's about the life span of the Ex-POW Association. Our numbers are falling off very quickly. We've got roughly around two hundred POWs left here, and when I took over as state secretary, we had about six hundred. Their average age would be about seventy-nine, I guess, but there's plenty well into their eighties.

I'm more concerned these days with the widows. They want to remain in their own homes, which is a big problem, and it's costly to go into nursing homes as well. Some of them have no family. Those who have a family who are responsible, they're alright, because their families will see them right. But you'd be surprised how many of them have children who are not interested in their mothers any longer. It's sad, you know.

If I see that they've got problems, I can only steer them in the right direction and say, 'Well look, I'll get in touch with the Veterans' Advice Network at DVA.' Fortunately, I've got a very good ally with the Deputy Commissioner of DVA in this state. We're good friends really. I don't go to her with any little thing – it's got to be a genuine case.

I think you're only as old as you feel. If you start thinking, 'Well, I'm eighty, I've got to slow down,' or if the wife, family, or other people say, 'You better slow down,' you say, 'Why do I want to slow down?' If I can keep going, I'll keep going, and I think it's better to be that way than to stop. The moment you stop because you *think* you're old, you've reached the point of no return.

So it doesn't bother me, you know. I don't even think about it, and I hope I'm not going to die for a long time, but I don't think about that either, whereas a lot of people say, 'Oh well, I'm at the end of the road.' I've had plenty of them say to me: 'I'm ready to go. I'm not a bit concerned.' But life's still precious to me, and I think I can still contribute a bit yet.

My theory is that it's better to wear out than to rust out.

CONCLUSION

The adjectives that we would use to describe the men, whose stories you have just read, are all positive – 'vital', 'stimulating', 'productive', 'enthusiastic'. There is wisdom evident within the stories about how to age 'well', as reflected in their living experiences. It is our opinion that although some of these men are in the public eye more than is usual for older men, stories of positive ageing are not uncommon among Australian men.

As every life and every story of ageing is unique, here we discuss the intriguing diversity of the stories. 'Ageing well' can mean different things to different people, but similarities and connections can be helpful, so we will also discuss the commonalties in the twelve stories.

As explained in our introduction, our interpretations of the interviews have been guided by negotiation with each of the men as to what would be included in his story.

Our interpretations may differ from those that you have made when reading and thinking about the stories. We all read through our own 'lens' on life – experiences, philosophies, belief systems, cultural influences, and other factors. We may 'see' different meanings, and we may learn from thinking about the interpretations of others. After all, we learn about life not only through observation, experience, and personal reflection, but also by listening to others. Indeed, the three of us in the project team are quite different in many ways, and at times our opinions varied about what were the relevant points and themes within the stories. Through listening to each other, and through discussion, we gained further insights, and eventually we reached a consensus.

BEING A DOER

Time and time again in interview, the men focused upon what they had done, but more emphatically, upon what they are still doing. To them it is very important to remain active. They are involved in many different activities: horse breeding, writing, story-telling, being an elder in a cultural group, winemaking, working for global health, fish-mongering, leading a religious community, welding, keeping fit, tutoring, caring for another, leading a movement, gardening, and helping others. There are also many other tangential or secondary activities mentioned.

Linked with this aim of remaining a 'doer' is the importance of doing what they want to do, and what they most enjoy doing. If their present main activity is not their top priority, perhaps because they are yet to retire, then they are planning to later become engaged in that priority. Some are continuing to work at what had been their previous occupation or profession, but perhaps now they have a narrower focus – one in which they are particularly interested, or to which they are committed. Others are focused upon an enjoyable and consuming hobby. Sometimes the previous and present work focus is their hobby! Often there is artistic activity or creativity. For instance, this may be story-telling, spear-making, writing verse, painting, music, making fine wine, or preparing tomato sauce.

In the doing, occasional elements of being an entrepreneur

are discernible, whether this is developing a symbiotic relationship with grape-growers or fishermen, or bringing good jazz to Australia. If they are pioneers in certain areas they tend to retain a connection with that activity.

There was considerable discussion about when they knew it was, or will know it is, time to stop being a full-time doer and become a part-time doer. This may be when 'retirement' occurs, but there are hazy boundaries concerning what they consider is retirement or semi-retirement. It is probably more appropriate to talk about moving from doing something full-time for financial gain, to doing something part-time for some or no financial gain. Half of the men chose to discuss when they would probably move to doing very little – but still they hope to be doing something! Two stated that they do not intend to move into the 'doing little' stage.

Half of the men have 'handed over' their previous business or work to younger men, who were usually, but not always, from their family. Although considerable control had been relinquished, it may be that some sense of ownership lingers, or perhaps the emotional connection continues. Four of the men continue to work with their son or sons. All these men unequivocally voiced their approval and pride in the success of the younger generation with the business or line of activity.

Two men talked about the tension that existed for them between doing and relaxing, and a number of the men explained how they, through prioritising, had let other activities lapse, such as recreation or church attendance. Several have to travel considerable distances in the line of their work, which is time-consuming. Three of the men spoke about the continuing sense of urgency regarding the need to 'get things done'. The attitudes to these aspects vary from pragmatic acceptance, to some regret.

Overall, only doing what you want to do and what you enjoy doing are resounding themes in the stories. We found it particularly illuminating that, in the interviews, if the discussion moved to question whether wisdom comes with age, there was often an immediate linking of wisdom with doing. Examples are, the wisdom to not hurt oneself when doing things, being better able to plan how and when to do things, and to know what to do and what not to do in regard to practical situations. Especially valued is the ability to effectively plan for successful outcomes.

However, this emphasis on doing what you enjoy is not necessarily a self-centred approach to life, as generally the activities the men most want to do are useful to others. They often significantly contribute to the well-being of their family, community, nation, or even the world.

FIGHTING BATTLES

'Older man as warrior' is not a common image, yet some of the men talked about the need to engage in battles. This is not the amusing bungling of a 'Dad's Army'. The good fight could be effectively negotiating bureaucracy, or campaigning against unsound political decisions and unjust forces.

The 'causes' to which the men have a commitment, and for which they go into battle, include the rights of ex-prisoners of war and their widows; adequate care of the veteran community, honouring agreements with grape-growers; the prevention of excessive and oppressive tax; global elimination of iodine deficiency brain damage in babies; Australians for a Constitutional Monarchy; the plight of refugees; the provision of adequate water supplies in a rural area; and the needs of people in emergency situations.

Considerable effort and time may be invested in the

battle. At least three of the men spoke about their motivation being at least partly derived from a Christian compassion for others. The words used in the interviews when explaining the need to fight were often those that communicate an emphatic and passionate attitude. Sometimes they spoke about how hard the battles are.

Regarding battles of another kind, three of the men had been in the armed services during the second world war. Two were in combat roles. Both discussed their thoughts now, as older men, about that earlier era, but neither spends much time reflecting on war experiences. They prefer to leave it behind them – to move on. Each tell of a specific meeting with Japanese people in more recent years that indicates a healing process has occurred, some time removed from those war battles.

BEING PHYSICALLY ACTIVE

Two thirds of these men are engaged in planned physical exercise. For some it is a prudent effort to prevent ill health and to keep relatively mobile, trim and fit. So they engage in exercise ranging from a daily exercise routine at home, to playing golf, or being a member of a fitness group.

For others of the men, the shock of a serious illness, or the onset of a potentially crippling disease, has impressed the need for regular exercise upon them. It seems that health trouble may often have prompted these men to consider the ageing process, and what to do differently. The experience of heart-related chest pain, and the diagnosis of serious heart disease requiring surgery, have been major promoters of exercise, as has the incidence of cancer. Their selection of exercise includes gardening, mowing lawns, daily walking, exercising specific limbs, and attending a gym.

A number of the men 'are up and at it' first thing in the

morning, some being very early risers indeed. Some have to force themselves to do the exercise, but either they prefer the exercise regime to the alternative of illness, pain, or earlier death, or else they motivate themselves by thinking that the exercise permits them to eat as they like. Alternatively, one man looks forward to his daily walk and regrets not having regularly walked earlier, before heart problems occurred.

A few seem to relish taking risks whilst exercising or engaging in recreational activities. Riding a motorbike and white-water rafting are two examples of potentially dangerous physical activities – not only for older men.

Exceptions exist. Taking virtually no exercise is also evident. Overall though, the men acknowledge the reality of some diminishment in physical strength, do not particularly like this, and thus see the need for exercise. The primary principle of doing what you want to do, and what you enjoy, is at play in this area of life also.

BEING MENTALLY ACTIVE

These men seem to value mental acuity probably more than remaining physically active. Collectively though, they seem to be accepting of a failing memory for things like names. Some are quite philosophical about the ability to remember events long past in great detail, yet having to struggle to recall recent events. However, there is considerable evidence of the men recognising a need to stay mentally active to prevent their cognitive reasoning diminishing.

Just as the shock of illness has jolted many of the men into exercising, or, for one man, an embarrassing fall prompting the use of a walking stick, so the distress resulting from a mental lapse can cause the men to seek a way to keep their mind active. One man experienced falling asleep in the early afternoon during a meeting – and then realising, on reflection, that his afternoon decision-making was not always well-reasoned. Consequently this man altered his daily schedule to include a brief after-lunch nap, which has resulted in improved performance for the remainder of the afternoon. Eight of the men take midday or afternoon naps, but at least one other finds absolutely no need to do so.

One coping mechanism mentioned to compensate for failing memory involves becoming super-organised – writing notes, carefully keeping a diary, or ensuring that another person, such as a wife or secretary, helps with organisation. However, the men also often spoke about the importance of using and exercising the mind. For instance, the University of the Third Age (U3A) is considered a way of not only staying mentally alert, but also of exploring topics about which you may have always been curious. A couple of the men were looking forward to further reading about, or studying, subjects in which they are interested – history, theology, art and the philosophy of ideas. Teaching others is another route suggested for mental invigoration.

The mental function of older relatives sometimes was briefly mentioned, either in regard to having retained mental faculties, or else the loss of such. Possibly the men are evaluating their risk of either outcome occurring for them.

NOTICING TIME PASSING

Overall there is awareness that time is passing. For some, there is a wistfulness for earlier times. This varies in focus, including the time when: Aboriginal men were strong and not weakened by alcohol; there was a flourishing racing industry in SA; law and order prevailed in society; sport was non-sponsored; fish were plentiful; and home-cooked food was both prolific and valued. Occasional mention was made of changing social norms including: the tendency to have children at a later age; children being born outside marriage; younger Greek Australians not celebrating 'name days'; and children watching television rather than playing outside.

The majority of men introduced the topic of death at some stage in the interview. Discussion on this topic included speculation about heaven, and funeral planning, such as the selection of music.

Two thirds of the men have assessed the tendency for longevity in their family. Several of the men have not only lived considerably longer than their fathers, but have also out-lived siblings, or not developed the health problems that have befallen siblings. These matters are of interest to the men, and sometimes are cause for speculation. A few of the men expressed amazement about having reached their present age. Some are very aware that death, especially sudden death, is not restricted to just older men, but that middle-aged men are at risk too. Although one man mentioned that statistically death is becoming less common for middle-aged men, another mentioned that his fellow Aboriginal men are not living as long as they used to.

With time passing, the men also have an interest in the future. One or two are hoping to reach a milestone, like living into the next century. There is curiosity as to what the future may bring for their main interest in life, coupled with either confidence or considerable concern about the sustainability of an industry or institution.

However, it was common for the men to say that they really didn't think about whether they were old, or getting old. It just happens. Although most of the men are of the opinion that not thinking about ageing arises from a positive attitude, one man actually considers this to be potentially dangerous, as being in a state of denial may decrease the openness to making adjustments that will enhance health and increase longevity.

SEEKING PLEASURE

Health is an ideal for many of the men, but at least five of them are not prepared to sacrifice pleasure for health. If there is something that they really like doing, which may be eating certain types of food, or smoking cigarettes, then they may keep on doing that. This factor varies however, with others of the men being quite willing to forgo unhealthy pleasure in the interests of good health.

Likewise, some men are teetotallers, others enjoy alcohol, and in particular a glass or two of red wine, which they link to good health. There is also considerable contrast between the men's attitude to food. Eating is obviously a top pleasure for about four of the men, and not so much with others. Whilst most have good appetites, some are very controlled in their eating compared to others.

Many of the men apparently appreciate having excitement in life. Apart from motorbike riding and white-water rafting, excitement was derived from foals dropping in spring, vintage in the Barossa Valley, gambling, meeting deadlines for publishers, watching hunting, being a sports fan, and going on four-wheel driving expeditions.

Travel may be very enjoyable. A couple of the men love driving. Since ceasing full-time work for financial gain, many have made the effort to 'see Australia', and all except one have travelled overseas, some doing so quite extensively. There is often a favourite holiday destination – maybe a yearly or regular place for retreat from a busy life. Three like to go fishing somewhere along the coast of South Australia. For others, travel was enjoyed in the past, but now they prefer to stay home, or closer to home.

At home, many of the men enjoy reading books, newspapers, or even poetry. Three of the men write poetry, others prefer the joy of tending a garden, including growing vegetables and exotic fruits. Painting may bring pleasure, as may art in various forms. Music is a great source of enjoyment for many of the men. One has spent virtually a lifetime bringing Australians to know and love jazz – his passion for jazz is not diminished. Choir conducting has been an activity of another in his later years, as well as earlier in life, and others prefer to have music constantly playing in their environment.

VALUING RELATIONSHIPS

Australian men tend to enjoy the company of their mates. This may be in a fish market, at the racetrack, in a gym, at the weighbridge of a winery, or at reunions. Otherwise, for these men, being with mates may occur through fishing or golfing trips, attending a fitness or painting group, 'sitting down' with other older Aboriginal people in different camps, going four-wheel driving in the bush, or organising card-games. Helping mates is also seen as important, whether it's welding or providing company. However, not all of the men make mateship a priority in their lives.

A more universal trait across this group of men is valuing their family, especially their wives. One is a widower, one regularly visits his wife in a nursing home, and the other ten live with their wives. Some of these relationships are second marriages. In general, they spoke with much appreciation and fondness about their wives, grateful both for their support and their contribution to family life – not only now, but also in the past. Some of the men chose to regretfully acknowledge that, as younger men, they had been so involved with their careers that their wives had been left with most of the responsibility of child rearing. There was mention of, in these latter years, a renewed appreciation of children. Having a good relationship with their children is a common aim, with family closeness and harmony appreciated. Regular family get-togethers are especially enjoyed. Sometimes considerable travel is necessary for this to occur. Living near their families was valued, although at least one man saw benefits in not living too close.

It was interesting that when some of the men were asked to describe their relationship with their grandchildren, there was apparent difficulty in defining the role. In contrast, others were very able to clearly explain what it was like being a grandfather, and readily articulated why grandchildren were important to them, and hopefully, vice versa. Without exception, however, the men prized their grandchildren.

The men often mentioned parents, grandparents, and members of their wider families. This was usually done with fondness and nostalgia. Some reflected upon how these family members had influenced their lives. There were occasional references to family roots, and for these men, their heritage appears to be important. They have visited places overseas that are their ancestral homes or land. Both of the immigrants to Australia have returned to their previous countries for visits, but they emphasised the rightness of moving to Australia. In the main though, the men seem to find it very important to either have, or be planning to have, a 'place' where they most want to live, and that is their own. Homes, gardens, and surrounds are important. One man values continuing to live in the family home with the myriad of memories that doing so evokes.

Some of the men have a great affinity with the land or sea – or with nature in general. The relationship with the land is of course particularly strong for the Aboriginal man, but several of the other men have respectfully observed the practice of landcare, or custodianship.

Relationship to God, or in a broader sense, spirituality, varies considerably. Mention was made of the spiritual and healing aspect of nature. Some of the men spoke about their Christianity and the positive influence which that has upon them, and the way in which they live their lives. Not all of the Christians regularly attend church, although they still retain a connection with the church. One man found that spirituality can be found through interacting with other people. The Aboriginal man has his Dreaming and sacred business and others have no religious affinity or spiritual inclination.

Several of the men think that you become anti-social as you age. Their experience is that they prefer to keep in touch with a small group of close friends and enjoy the pleasures of home and family more than attending parties, clubs and the like. In contrast, others seek social interaction and are active members of clubs. Mixing with different generations is valued, with children thought of fondly. Some men have interacted with three generations in their line of work over the years.

Over half of the men introduced the topic of medical care. They spoke admirably about their medical advisers and specialists, and obviously some of the men have appreciative relationships with these doctors, especially their general practitioners.

A few of the men discussed wanting to think well of others, and a reluctance to be uncharitable toward people. A few remarked about how, as older men, their expectations of others are now more realistic, more compassionate, and they have an increased understanding leading to tolerance. This may include a much more balanced view about life.

Ample evidence can be found in all the stories about the value of communicating with other people, whether this is family and close friends, or perhaps with a wider circle of acquaintances – or even perhaps a readership. Overall, relationships and continuing communication with others are of primary importance. Some spoke definitely and appreciably about feeling loved – and having others to love.

KNOWING WHO I AM

The men appreciate being of an age where they experience the strength and assurance of knowing who they are. One of them stated that mature people know this by the time they turn fifty. Now they have a sense of consistency in their identity. For these men, this identity is mostly tied with what they have done, and what they continue to do, but it can be more complex than that. It can be connected with their race and culture, or with membership of an influential family.

Closely associated with this knowing oneself, is the notion of status. Some are aware of their international status, and the accompanying responsibility. Others have national or local status, including the status of 'elder' in a community. Status may be more practical, such as being 'the provider' for a family – and having assured that, following his death, his wife and family will be financially secure. Two of the men are patrons of organisations. With status there may be 'influence', or the knowledge of being a respected member of their community.

This strong sense of identity is reinforced when the men are sought by family, friends and colleagues for their advice. The men are happy to provide advice, and it gives them a sense of being valued as older men with experience. A few of the men continue to hold significant leadership positions – and they are comfortable with that responsibility.

187

With this knowing of self, a type of relaxed sense of humour is discernible. These men like to laugh, and are comfortable laughing at themselves. They don't necessarily take life or themselves too seriously!

Some of the men expressed a strong sense of continuity of self. This is evident from individual statements that explain feeling mentally about fifteen, always thinking that you are young, thinking that you are the same, being at heart still the same person, and not feeling any different than they did when they were much younger.

In different ways, the men feel as if they have been, and are, fortunate. This feeling is variously connected to having travel opportunities, meeting interesting people, being happily married, still having mental acuity, one's work being sought, not having cardiac problems, being involved with meaningful and useful work, being appreciated, having a loving family, getting good 'breaks' in life, moving to live in Australia, experiencing good health, and in living so long.

Interestingly, some of the men volunteered information about either not being scholars, or else explaining what they were like as a student at school. There seems to be some reflection occurring about their academic abilities in regard to the opportunities in life that they did not receive, or that they chose not to take.

However, most of the men are satisfied with life as an older man. This was expressed in various ways, including being at peace with the world, having accomplished what they wanted, and being pleased with success regarding a worthy cause. Some of the men declared that since 'retirement' they have experienced the most satisfying, rewarding, or productive part of their life. Within all of this, the constant common denominator is that they are doing what they want to do, and that which they most enjoy. Overall, they see themselves as 'doers'.

HAVING AN OPINION ON AGEING

You would have noticed that some of the men have adages they live by, but within their stories there is also advice about how to age well. Most are of the opinion that this may be a very individual matter, and their advice may not be suitable for other men. Despite this, there are some similarities among the advice offered.

Not worrying is emphasised, particularly concerning health. Linked to this is the importance of leaving things behind that may be upsetting. Forgiving others for past wrongs is encouraged. However, living in the present is what matters, and not dwelling on the past. The past is past. Recalling good memories is encouraged, so long as you are focused mostly on the present, and don't talk too much about the old times. Keep alert, be mentally active and interested in things around you, and in what is happening in the world. Keep communicating with others, and don't let your world get smaller and smaller – communication is considered essential for a sense of wellness. Also, some advocate minimising weight gain.

The men are hopeful that older people's contributions to the community will be increasingly recognised. According to the men, the talents of older people should be appreciated and put to use, the government should focus on encouraging their input, and more effort should be made to prevent the social isolation of the aged.

The strongest and most common advice, however, is to not sit down and do nothing. It is essential not to 'throw in the towel'; not to pull a rug over your knees and wait for the end. Don't let your footprints get sedentary. It is vital that you never 'give up' and have an easy life. The men say that they can see a big difference between people they know who have done this compared with others who are remaining active and busy. Comment was made about the need to keep working hard for your cause. This then leads to the major theme of this book, and thus its title . . . Still doing, never done.